AN ANTHOLOGY OF POST-COLONIAL POETRY

Edited by

V. R. BADIGER |

AKKAMAHADEVI P.

Late. Sri. Parashuramappa Achar & Late. Eshwaramma B.

Contents

Contents

Contents

Contents

Contents

Contents

Contents

Contents

Contents

Contents

Contents

Contents

Author's Note

V.R.Badiger, now aged 66, is a retired Professor of English from Dept of English, Gulbarga University, Kalaburagi, in north Karnataka. Totally, he put in 39 years of teaching English and English literatures in undergraduate and post-graduate levels. His main areas of research was Anglo-Indian Literature and Modern British Literature in India, he was forced to teach Phonetics and Linguistics. Already he published 14 books. He has three children of which the first two daughters, Swetha B.E., and Dr Sujatha MBBS, got educated and employed and he lives with his wife, Dr.Akkamahadevi and son, Santoshkumar, MBA in Kalaburagi.

Foreword

Nowadays the hard copy book is less relevant in the classroom as the teacher and students depend on the mobile use- google temporarily. Whatever it is in the google they teach and learn. *An Anthology of Commonwealth Poetry* edited by C.D.Narasimaiah is one good anthology available but it had no supplementary information. Sometimes, we do not understand whether somebody is a poet or poetess. It is a mere collection of poems. There are no biographical details about the poets of the various countries. In that direction Prof.VR.Badiger has thought to bring some improvement upon the earlier and come out with this revised and updated edition with changed title -*An Anthology of Post-Colonial Poetry* that includes, in addition, the colonial poetry also.

This humble academic attempt made by him must be well appreciated by the teachers and students who study post-colonial literature and poetry, in particular. With all my heart, I bless him for the work he has done and it is welcome contribution to the field of tools of teaching in the classroom.

C. R. Yeravintelimath "Chaitra"
Emeritus Professor, Dharwar 583003

Preface

It is the day to day problem of a teacher at the post-graduate level to choose a text of post-colonial poetry for the students and teach the poems. There is but one available antholog,C.D.Narasimaiah edited- *An Anthology of Commonwealth Poetry* published by Macmillan, Madras. Except that old book which is left unrevised and unprinted for decades; there is no other text of its kind. The present edition is to be revised, in a sense, and made anew for the demands of the present day post-graduate students who study the post-colonial poetry.

Hence this humble attempt has been made to revise and update the old edition by adding photos of the poets and biogaraphical details and explanations; so that is shall be useful as a tool in the classroom.

We hereby duly acknowledge all earlier editors, authors and publishers, espcailly Macmillan India, Chennai who published Prof.C.D.Narasimahaih's edition.

V.R.Badiger & Akkamahadevi P.

INDIA

TORU DUTT (1856-1877)

Toru Dutt was sent to England for education at the early age. There she studied French and wrote poetry in French and published her poems. She also translated some of the French into English. She is well-known as poet and translator. Her main works are- *A Sheaf Gleaned in the French Fields* and *Ancient Balladsand Legends of Hindustan.*

1. Sonnet-The Lotus

Love came to Flora asking for a flower
That would of flowers be undisputed queen,
The lily and the rose, long, long had been
Rivals for that high honour. Bards of power
Had sung their claims. "The rose can never tower
Like the pale lily with her Juno mien"—
"But is the lily lovelier?" Thus between
Flower-factions rang the strife in Psyche's bower.
Give me a flower delicious as the rose
And stately as the lily in her pride"—
But of what colour?"—"Rose-red," Love first chose,
"Then prayed,—"No, lily-white,—or, both provide;"
And Flora gave the lotus, "rose-red" dyed,
And "lily-white,"—the queenliest flower that blows.

2. Our Casuarina Tree

Like a huge Python, winding round and round
The rugged trunk, indented deep with scars,
Up to its very summit near the stars,
A creeper climbs, in whose embraces bound
No other tree could live. But gallantly
The giant wears the scarf, and flowers are hung
In crimson clusters all the boughs among,
Whereon all day are gathered bird and bee;
And oft at nights the garden overflows
With one sweet song that seems to have no close,
Sung darkling from our tree, while men repose.
When first my casement is wide open thrown
At dawn, my eyes delighted on it rest;
Sometimes, and most in winter,—on its crest
A gray baboon sits statue-like alone
Watching the sunrise; while on lower boughs
His puny offspring leap about and pl
And far and near kokilas hail the day;
And to their pastures wend our sleepy cows;
And in the shadow, on the broad tank cast
By that hoar tree, so beautiful and vast,
The water-lilies spring, like snow enmassed.
But not because of its magnificence
Dear is the Casuarina to my soul:
Beneath it we have played; though years may roll,
O sweet companions, loved with love intense,
For your sake, shall the tree be ever dear.
Blent with your images, it shall arise
In memory, till the hot tears blind mine eyes!

What is that dirge-like murmur that I hear
Like the sea breaking on a shingle-beach?
It is the tree's lament, an eerie speech,
That haply to the unknown land may reach.
Unknown, yet well-known to the eye of faith!
Ah, I have heard that wail far, far away
In distant lands, by many a sheltered bay,
When slumbered in his cave the water-wraith
And the waves gently kissed the classic shore
Of France or Italy, beneath the moon,
When earth lay trancèd in a dreamless swoon:
And every time the music rose,—before
Mine inner vision rose a form sublime,
Thy form, O Tree, as in my happy prime
I saw thee, in my own loved native clime.
Therefore I fain would consecrate a lay
Unto thy honor, Tree, beloved of those
Who now in blessed sleep for aye repose,—
Dearer than life to me, alas, were they!
Mayst thou be numbered when my days are done
With deathless trees—like those in Borrowdale,
Under whose awful branches lingered pale
"Fear, trembling Hope, and Death, the skeleton,
And Time the shadow;" and though weak the verse
That would thy beauty fain, oh, fain rehearse,
May Love defend thee from Oblivion's curse.

SRI AUROBINDO (1872-1950)

He was a revolutionary, studied in England for the ICS and later involved in the freedom movement against the British. After a bomb-blast case he was jailed but he escaped to Pondicherry where in he established an ashram. He became a famous mystic, poet, writer, critic, and essayist. His main works are- *Savitri*, *The Human Cycle*, *The Renaissance in India* and *The Future Poetry* etc.

3. The Pilgrim of the Night

I made an assignation with the Night;
In the abyss was fixed our rendezvous:
In my breast carrying God's deathless light
I came her dark and dangerous heart to woo.
I left the glory of the illumined Mind
And the calm rapture of the divinised soul
And travelled through a vastness dim and blind
To the grey shore where her ignorant waters roll.
I walk by the chill wave through the dull slime
And still that weary journeying knows no end;
Lost is the lustrous godhead beyond Time,
There comes no voice of the celestial Friend.
And yet I know my footprints' track shall be
A pathway towards Immortality.

4. The Stone Goddess

In a town of gods, housed in a little shrine,
From sculptured limbs, the Godhead looked at me,–
A living Presence deathless and divine,
A Form that harbored all infinity.
The great World Mother and her mighty will
Inhabited the earth's abysmal sleep,
Voiceless, omnipotent, inscrutable,
Mute in the desert and the sky and deep.
Now veiled with mind she dwells and speaks no word,
Voiceless, inscrutable, omniscient,
Hiding until our soul has seen, has heard
The secret of her strange embodiment,
One in the worshipper and the immobile shape,
A beauty and mystery flesh or stone can drape.

5. Surreal Science

One dreamed and saw a gland write Hamlet, drink
At the Mermaid, capture immortality;
A committee of hormones on the Aegean's brink
Composed the Iliad and the Odyssey.
A thyroid, meditating almost nude
Under the Bo-tree, saw the eternal Light
And, rising from its mighty solitude,
Spoke of the Wheel and eight-fold Path all right.
A brain by a disordered stomach driven
Thundered through Europe, conquered, ruled and fell;
From St. Helena went, perhaps, to Heaven.
Thus wagged on the surreal world, until
A scientist played with atoms and blew out
The universe before God had time to shout.

6. Despair on the Staircase

Mute stands she, lonely on the topmost stair,
An image of magnificent despair;
The grandeur of a sorrowful surmise
Wakes in the largeness of her glorious eyes.
In her beauty's dumb significant pose I find
The tragedy of her mysterious mind.
Yet is she stately, grandiose, full of grace.
A musing mask is her immobile face.
Her tail is up like an unconquered flag;
Its dignity knows not the right to wag.
An animal creature wonderfully human,
A charm and miracle of fur-footed Brahman,
Whether she is spirit, woman or a cat,
Is now the problem I am wondering at.

SAROJINI NAIDU (1879-1949)

She was an Indian political activist and poetess. A proponent of civil rights, women's emancipation and ach- imperialism she played a vital role in the Indian independence movement against the British. Her main works are- *The Village Song,*(1902) *ThePalanquinBearers, TheGoldenThreshold*(1905) and *TheBrokenWings-Songs*(1917).

7. Indian Weavers

Weavers, weaving at break of day,
Why do you weave a garment so gay?
Blue as the wing of a halcyon wild,
We weave the robes of a new-born child.
Weavers, weaving at fall of night,
Why do you weave a garment so bright?
Like the plumes of a peacock, purple and green,
We weave the marriage-veils of a queen.
Weavers, weaving solemn and still,
What do you weave in the moonlight chill?
White as a feather and white as a cloud,
We weave a dead man's funeral shroud.

8. Song of Radha, The Milkmaid

I carried my curds to the Mathura fair …
How softly the heifers were lowing …
I wanted to cry, "Who will buy
These curds that are white as the clouds in the sky
When the breezes of shrawan are blowing?"
But my heart was so full of your beauty, Beloved,
They laughed as I cried without knowing:
Govinda! Govinda!
Govinda! Govinda!
How softly the river was flowing
I carried my pots to the Mathura tide …
How gaily the rowers were rowing! …
My comrades called, "Ho! let us dance, let us sing
And wear saffron garments to welcome the spring.
And pluck the new buds that are blowing."
But my heart was so full of your music, Beloved,
They mocked when I cried without knowing:
Govinda! Govinda!
Govinda! Govinda!
How gaily the river was flowing!
I carried my gifts to the Mathura shrine …
How brightly the torches were glowing! …
I folded my hands at the altars to pray
"O shining ones guard us by night and by day"—
And loudly the conch shells were blowing.
But my heart was so lost in your worship, Beloved,
They were wroth when I cried without knowing:
Govinda! Govinda!
Govinda! Govinda!

How brightly the river was flowing

SHIV K. KUMAR (1921-2017)

Born in Lahore in present Pakistan, in 1921, he became an Indian English poet,playwright novelist and shot story writer. His grandfather late Tulsi Das Kumar was a school teacher and his father Bishan Das Kumar was a retired head master. Later 'K' stands for Krishna.i.e., Shiv Krishna Kumar. Of his several collections, his master piece *Trapfalls in the Sky* which won him the Sahitya Akademi award for his literary contribution to Indian English literature.

9. Indian Women

In this triple-baked continent
women don't etch angry eyebrows
on mud walls.
Patiently they sit
like empty pitchers
on the mouth of the village well
pleating hope in each braid of their mississippi-long hair
looking deep into the water's mirror
for the moisture in their eyes.
With zodiac doodlings on the sands
they guard their tattooed thighs
Waiting for their men's return
till even the shadows
roll up their contours and are gone beyond the hills.

NISSIM EZEKIEL (1924-2004)

Belonging to Jewish community Nissim Ezekiel was born and bred up in Mumbai. He became a professor of English in the University of Mumbai. He was also a poet, playwright and art-critic and editor. He was a famous modern Indian English poet known for use of irony. His main works are- *Nightof the Scorpion , Latter Day Psalms.*

10. Enterprise

It started as a pilgrimage
Exalting minds and making all
The burdens light, The second stage
Explored but did not test the call.
The sun beat down to match our rage.
We stood it very well, I thought ,
Observed and put down copious notes
On things the peasants sold and bought
The way of serpents and of goats.
Three cities where a sage had taught .
But when the differences arose
On how to cross a desert patch,
We lost a friend whose stylish prose
Was quite the best of all our batch.
A shadow falls on us and grows.
Another phase was reached when we
Were twice attacked, and lost our way.
A section claimed its liberty
To leave the group. I tried to pray .
Our leader said he smelt the sea.
We noticed nothing as we went,
A straggling crowd of little hope,
Ignoring what the thunder meant,
Deprived of common needs like soap.
Some were broken, some merely bent.
When, finally , we reached the place ,
We hardly know why we were there.
The trip had darkened every face,
Our deeds were neither great nor rare.

Home is where we have to gather grace.

11. Night of the Scorpion

I remember the night my mother
was stung by a scorpion. Ten hours
of steady rain had driven him
to crawl beneath a sack of rice.
Parting with his poison - flash
of diabolic tail in the dark room -
he risked the rain again.
The peasants came like swarms of flies
and buzzed the name of God a hundred times
to paralyze the Evil One.
With candles and with lanterns
throwing giant scorpion shadows
on the mud-baked walls
they searched for him: he was not found.
They clicked their tongues.
With every movement that the scorpion made
his poison moved in
Mother's blood, they said.
May he sit still, they said
May the sins of your previous birth
be burned away tonight, they said.
May your suffering decrease
the misfortunes of your next birth, they said.
May the sum of all evil
balanced in this unreal world
against the sum of good
become diminished by your pain.
May the poison purify your flesh
of desire, and your spirit of ambition,

they said, and they sat around
on the floor with my mother in the centre,
the peace of understanding on each face.
More candles, more lanterns, more neighbours,
more insects, and the endless rain.
My mother twisted through and through,
groaning on a mat.
My father, sceptic, rationalist,
trying every curse and blessing,
powder, mixture, herb and hybrid.
He even poured a little paraffin
upon the bitten toe and put a match to it.
I watched the flame feeding on my mother.
I watched the holy man perform his rites
to tame the poison with an incantation.
After twenty hours
it lost its sting.
My mother only said
Thank God the scorpion picked on me
And spared my children...

12. Goodbye Party for Miss Pushpa T.S

Friends,
our dear sister
is departing for foreign
in two three days,
and
we are meeting today
to wish her bon voyage.
You are all knowing, friends,
What sweetness is in Miss Pushpa.
I don't mean only external sweetness
but internal sweetness.
Miss Pushpa is smiling and smiling
even for no reason but simply because
she is feeling.
Miss Pushpa is coming
from very high family.
Her father was renowned advocate
in Bulsar or Surat,
I am not remembering now which place.
Surat? Ah, yes,
once only I stayed in Surat
with family members
of my uncle's very old friend-
his wife was cooking nicely...
that was long time ago.
Coming back to Miss Pushpa
she is most popular lady

with men also and ladies also.
Whenever I asked her to do anything,
she was saying, 'Just now only
I will do it.' That is showing
good spirit. I am always
appreciating the good spirit.
Pushpa Miss is never saying no.
Whatever I or anybody is asking
she is always saying yes,
and today she is going
to improve her prospect
and we are wishing her bon voyage.
Now I ask other speakers to speak
and afterwards Miss Pushpa
will do summing up.

JAYANTH MAHAPATRA (1928-2024)

Jayanth Mahapatra was an Indian English poet belonging to Orissa. He was the first Indian poet to receive Sahitya Akademi award for his English poetry. His main works are- *Relationship* (1980), *Bare Face*, and *Shadow Space* and *The Dane of the Peacock*. He was awarded with Padmashri.

13. A Monsoon Day Fable

The fable at the beginning of the monsoon
echoes alone, like a bell ringing in a temple
far from home. The furrows of earth that turned
year after year do not change shape or colour:
is it music, this immortality? Crouching silence
that takes cover inside a lump of shadow.
simply mocking man? Suddenly the face of the girl
I cannot have appears before me.
And the tune of the latest hit song interrupts itself,
then resumes in my head. I think
of visiting the afternoon movie hoping to see
the ageing dancer who lives by herself across the street
I feel the silence of a woman's secret whiteness
where her petticoat, loose and undone, lies open
sorrowfully, as though after an act of love.
I feel the silence of the ugly, squint-eyed girl
as she paces the street, between the taunting buildings.
All this adds up to a silence the meaning of which
I cannot reach; or was it a destiny, a fable,
a scent of the same rain on the earth?
Or the pull of a loose muscle in the dancer's startled leg?
The Cuttack dawn herds the emaciated cows
toward the municipal slaughter-house, their feet
slipping, their eyes following the vague light
into silence. Wet, as though with glue, they haunt
me through the nights, perhaps equipped with designs
to show man his true nature, perhaps
like the eyes of Einstein. For me to deny
the thought that I am in a sort of exile.

My observation is limited to the process of my falling,
and neither the law of falling bodies ·
nor the general theory of relativity stills the wing.
The day stands like a mature prime minister
bur a thousand thoughts away, a thousand voices above
the level of mournful lowing in my room.
I pick up the morning newspaper and see
how a nation goes on insulting itself
with its own web of rhetoric. And remember how
some of us poets had participated at the Silver Jubilee
celebrations of the Sahitya Akademi in New Delhi,
and with plagiarized smiles and abstract talk
convinced ourselves that in harmony there was
no deception. It seems so strange looking at one another
and finding ourselves go into the distances of our eyes;
even my wife does not look as if she belonged to me,
and even the spittle I swallow every hour
has nothing perhaps to do with me, like
that unreachable Girl who leads me to a dim corner
of my conscience, alone. Alone, I look at her
as though I do not understand, the heart dry
in the midst of all this wetness.
At dawn when rain scratches against my skin
I hear again that familiar beat which did noth1ng
but merely quicken for someone's presence,
and I hear the silence of today
in its song of dead refrains:
a lonely halo of earth
that gazes aimlessly about the footprintts
of someone going home.

14. The Lost Children of America

Here
in the dusty malarial lanes
of Cuttack where years have slowly lost their secrets
they wander
in these lanes nicked by intrigue and rain
and the unseen hands of gods
in front of a garish temple of the simian Hanuman
along river banks splattered with excreta and dung
in the crowded market square among rotting tomatoes
fish-scales and the moist warm odour of bananas
and piss
passing by the big-breasted, hard-eyed young whores
who frequent the empty space behind the local cinema
by the Town Hall where corrupt politicians still
go on delivering their pre-election speeches
and on the high road above the town's burning-ground
from which gluttonous tan smoke floats up
in the breeze, smacking of scorched marrow and doubt.
Here
like the unreal stirrings
of incense smoke in a darkened shrine
like the languid movements of mangled lepers
around a temple of the goddess Chandi at dawn
like a wounded whale drifting away
sadly in unknown seas
like the dark winds of Asia
which murmur joylessly in slums but do not answer
they wander, these lost children of America,
flaunting their long unkempt hair and their feet;

a man naked to the waist, the fringes
of his torn shorts two weary chapped mouths—
a woman, her face of old porcelain
burnt in the harsh sun
clothed indifferently in a discoloured sack
her breasts weak and sagging
having lost their glimmer and their power;
the lost children wander bare-eyed
smelling of incense and living on grass and flowers
like scavengers accompanied by their impassive shadows
perhaps in search of many gods, to ask for strength,
with their appearance of sibyls and witches,
limp and cold with the ablutions of another
separate world.
Or perhaps
like she-jackals pursued
by invisible hunters who retreat
with their wounded cubs into jungle depths,
and prompted by something stronger than fear
seek refuge in some forester's shack for succour
and for that fierce bond of air
or to find whether these tropic winds
would catch and belly out the sails of their minds
that have been woven
with the strands of sardonic guts.
No one knows them,
they are the free, the common men
soft and green of gesture, preoccupied
with their hidden songs of mankind,
mind blown by acid and amphetamines
and we watch them go by
with vague feelings of exaltation and disquiet.
They are the people we do not need to know:

they, for instance, do not travel as guests
of Rotary International or the UNO.
They are the lost children
who do not need to ask us oft-repeated questions:
Why is my skin so brown, my birth not final?
Why do I clean my arse with my hand?
Why do I seek a virgin woman for a wife?
Why do I grovel before that grotesque god
of bitter wood Ihave helped to carve?
And why do I seize wisdom from this swaddled sod?
I have no need to ask
why they come ten thousand miles,
for though their eyes are open they appear asleep,
and perhaps they too are men with dreams:
these men rushing through endless supermarket aisles,
the calligraphy of hallucinogens in their blue eyes,
the incredible flesh in whose innocence they hide,
the breathless thighs, the motor of the precious pubis:
harmless obsessions
that take them only for a ride.
And in desperate sleep they move their eyes
opening their hidden faces
like lonely picture postcards of unknown lands;
perhaps some sing, and some others
chant the mantras of the dead
with that benign resignation of all children,
or perhaps like victims waiting out
the relentlessness of time,
keep watching the skies with terror in their gaze.
For at the dusk's edge
blurred by the glare of unearthly flares
feebled by a sticky silence of faraway flutes
they learn to come to themselves

at the threshold of the void
as the emptiness of the sky's luminous bowl
fills their eyes with a single hue:
the colour of the Third Eye, the oblique, the great,
the colour of eyes when the light goes out of them
the colour of nakedness and of flayed skin,
and they recognize states of humiliation
and hunger and the well-being of a woman
drying herself with her only wet sari
after her bath, and the nameless solitude
that has nothing to hide behind,
no tragedies small or big,
and they find the secret of dying
without realizing that they are dying.
We gaze at each other in silence, the lost child and I;
who knows who is playing a joke on whom?
What can drive me from these mean, sordid alleys
where I live?
Who is the one among us misled by vision,
more real than real,
that has filled homes with tremulous ash
and has brought from hunger unassuaged
the haunted wood and the hunted myth?
In the Hanuman Temple last night
the priest's pomaded jean-clad son
raped the squint-eyed fourteen-year fisher girl
on the cracked stone platform behind the shrine
and this morning
her father found her at the police station
assaulted over and over again by four policemen
dripping of darkness and of scarlet death.
In this time of darknesses the lost ones and I
will dim like lamps and go back to the moments

we caught once in the uncertain light of dawns;
to balance ourselves in falsehood,
in the colour of dead leaves on the earth,
falling upon the unreal word of simile and metaphor,
glorying in hyperbole
as we wait to be allowed our manner of quieter joy,
and silencing the world with borrowed voices
of the dead that sing homage to clay
in crippling ennui:
echoes of an isolating idolatry.
And now we will endure the pain
when the words of our songs droop like lilies
in the dark without standing in judgement,
passing by the abandoned cocoon
through the stench of blood over the pure dawn wall
across the stinging smoke of burnt-out doubts:
perhaps like ageing men
in their bitter-lemon gaze who look up wearily
from their doorsteps when the truth-light of day
is levelling.
So to find the time among us,
here on earth
when history does not reverberate any more
with the pulse of the drum
or with the chant of the tide on a sacred Puri shore
but with the echoes of a bruised presence
lying like a stone
at the bottom of the soul's clear pool,
feeling the virtue that is there
in the refracted light, the earth-sense
of what pleases us and of what is lost
forever beyond us,
as the burden of ununderstood things billows upward

like smoke.

A. K. RAMANUJAN (1929- 1993)

He was an Indian scholar and a poet of Indian Literature and Dravidian Linguistics. He was born in-Mysore He was a professor of English in Lingaraj College, Belgaum and later in the University of Chicago. He was also a playwright , folklorist, and philologist . He got MacArthur award for his poetry.His main works are- *Song of Earth*(1968), *Speaking of Shiva* (1973) and *Hymns for the Drowning.*(1981*)*.

15. Love Poem for a Wife

Really what keeps us apart
at the end of years is unshared
childhood. You cannot, for instance,
meet my father. He is some years
dead. Neither can I meet yours:
he has lately lost his temper
and mellowed.
In the transverse midnight gossip
of cousins' reunions among
brandy fumes, cashews and the Absences
of grandparents, you suddenly grow
nostalgic for my past and I
envy you your village dog-ride
and the mythology
of the sever crazy aunts.
You begin to recognize me
as I pass from ghost to real
and back again in the albums
of family rumours, in brothers'
anecdotes of how noisily
father bathed,
slapping soap on his back;
find sources for a familiar
sheep-mouth look in a sepia wedding
picture of father in a turban,
mother standing on her bare
splayed feet, silver rings
on her second toes;
and reduce the entire career

of my recent unique self
to the compulsion of some high
sentence in His Smilesian diary.
And your father, gone irrevocably
in age, after changing every day
your youth's evenings,
he will acknowledge the wickedness
of no reminiscence: no, not
the burning end of the cigarette
in the balcony, pacing
to and fro as you came to the gate
late, after what you thought
was an innocent
date with a nice Muslim friend
who only hinted at touches.
Only two weeks ago, in Chicago,
you and your brother James started
one of you old drag-out fights
about where the bathroom was
in the backyard,
north or south of the well
next to the jackfruit tree
in your father's father's house
in Alleppey. Sister-in-law
and I were blank cut-outs
fitted to our respective
slots in a room
really nowhere as the two of you
got down to the floor to draw
blueprints of a house from memory
of everything, from newspapers
to the backs of envelopes
and road-maps of the United States

that happened
to flap in the other room
in a midnight wind: you wagered heirlooms
and husband's earnings on what the Uncle in Kuwait
would say about the Bathroom
and the Well, and the dying,
by now dead,
tree next to it. Probably
only the Egyptians had it right:
their kings had sisters for queens
to continue the incests
of childhood into marriage.
or we should do as well-meaning
Hindus did.
betroth us before birth
forestalling separate horoscopes
and mother's first periods,
and wed us in the oral cradle
and carry marriage back into
the namelessness of childhoods.

16. Small-scale Reflections on a Great House

Sometimes I think that nothing
that ever comes into this house
goes out. Things that come in everyday
to lose themselves among other things
lost long ago among
other things lost long ago;
lame wandering cows from nowhere
have been known to be tethered,
given a name, encouraged
to get pregnant in the broad daylight
of the street under the elders'
supervision, the girls hiding
behind windows with holes in them.
Unread library books
usually mature in two weeks
and begin to lay a row
of little eggs in the ledgers
for fines, as silverfish
in the old man's office room
breed dynasties among long legal words
in the succulence
of Victorian parchment.
Neighbours' dishes brought up
with the greasy sweets they made
all night the day before yesterday
for the wedding anniversary of a god,
never leave the house they enter,

like the servants, the phonographs,
the epilepsies in the blood,
sons-in-law who quite forget
their mothers, but stay to check
accounts or teach arithmetic to nieces,
or the women who come as wives
from houses open on one side
to rising suns, on another
to the setting, accustomed
to wait and to yield to monsoons
in the mountains' calendar
beating through the hanging banana leaves
And also anything that goes out
will come back, processed and often
with long bills attached,
like the hooped bales of cotton
shipped off to invisible Manchesters
and brought back milled and folded
for a price, cloth for our days'
middle-class loins, and muslin
for our richer nights. Letters mailed
have a way of finding their way back
with many re-directions to wrong
addresses and red ink-marks
earned in Tiruvalla and Sialkot.
And ideas behave like rumours,
once casually mentioned somewhere
they come back to the door as prodigies
born to prodigal fathers, with eyes
that vaguely look like our own,
like what Uncle said the other day:
that every Plotinus we read
is what some Alexander looted

between the malarial rivers.
A beggar once came with a violin
to croak out a prostitute song
that our voiceless cook sang
all the time in our backyard.
Nothing stays out: daughters
get married to short-lived idiots;
sons who run away come back
in grand children who recite Sanskrit
to approving old men, or bring
betel nuts for visiting uncles
who keep them gaping with
anecdotes of unseen fathers,
or to bring Ganges water
in a copper pot
for the last of the dying
ancestors' rattle in the throat.
And though many times from everywhere,
recently only twice:
once in nineteen-forty-three
from as far as the Sahara,
half -gnawed by desert foxes,
and lately from somewhere
in the north, a nephew with stripes
on his shoulder was called
an incident on the border
and was brought back in plane
and train and military truck
even before the telegrams reached,
on a perfectly good.

17. Obituary

Father, when he passed on,
left dust
on a table of papers,
left debts and daughters,
a bedwetting grandson
named by the toss
of a coin after him,
a house that leaned
slowly through our growing
years on a bent coconut
tree in the yard.
Being the burning type,
he burned properly
at the cremation
as before, easily
and at both ends,
left his eye coins
in the ashes that didn't
look one bit different,
several spinal discs, rough,
some burned to coal, for sons
to pick gingerly
and throw as the priest
said, facing east
where three rivers met
near the railway station;
no longstanding headstone
with his full name and two dates
to holdin their parentheses

everything he didn't quite
manage to do himself,
like his cesarian birth
in a brahmin ghetto
and his death by heart-
failure in the fruit market.
But someone told me
he got two lines
in an inside column
of a Madras newspaper
sold by the kilo
exactly four weeks later
to street hawkers
who sell it in turn
to the small groceries
where I buy salt,
coriander,
and jaggery
in newspaper cones
that I usually read
for fun, and lately
in the hope of finding
these obituary lines.
And he left us
a changed mother
and more than
one annual ritual.

18. Allama Prabhu

Poets of the past
Are the children of my concubines.
Poets to come
Are infants of my pity.
The poets of the sky
Are babies in my cradle.
Vishnu and Brahma
Are my kinsmen and sidekicks.
You are the father-on-law
And I the son-in-law.
O Lord of Caves

ARUN KOLATKAR (1932-2004)

He was a famous Indian poet belonging to Maharastra. He wrote both in Marathi and English. His poems found humour in everyday matters. He is the only Indian English poet other than Kabir to be featured on the World Classics titles of New York Review of Books. His main work is *Jejuri*, a long poem of pilgrimage. He published several collections of poems.

19. The Bus

The tarpaulin flaps are buttoned down
on the windows of the state transport bus.
all the way up to jejuri.
a cold wind keeps whipping
and slapping a corner of tarpaulin at your elbow.
you look down to the roaring road.
you search for the signs of daybreak in what
little light spills out of bus.
your own divided face in the pair of glasses
on an oldman's nose
is all the countryside you get to see.
you seem to move continually forward.
toward a destination
just beyond the castemark beyond his eyebrows.
outside, the sun has risen quitely
it aims through an eyelet in the tarpaulin.
and shoots at the oldman's glasses.
a sawed off sunbeam comes to rest gently
against the driver's right temple.
the bus seems to change direction.
at the end of bumpy ride with your own face
on the either side
when you get off the bus.
you don't step inside the old man's head.

20. An Old Woman

An old woman grabs
hold of your sleeve
and tags along.
She wants a fifty paise coin.
She says she will take you
to the horseshoe shrine.
You've seen it already.
She hobbles along anyway
and tightens her grip on your shirt
She won't let you go.
You know how old women are.
They stick to you like a burr.
You turn around and face her
with an air of finality.
You want to end the farce.
When you hear her say,
'What else can an old woman do
on hills as wretched as these?'
You look right at the sky.
Clear through the bullet holes
she has for her eyes.
And as you look on,
the cracks that begin around her eyes
spread beyond her skin.
And the hills crack.
And the temples crack.
And the sky falls
With a plateglass clatter
around the shatterproof crone

who stands alone.
And you are reduced
to so much small change
in her hand.

21. Chaitanya

'Sweet as grapes
Are the stones of Jejuri',
Said Chaitanya.
He popped a stone
In his mouth
And spat out gods.

22. Makarand

Take my shirt off
and go in there to do puja ?
No thanks.
Not me.
But you go right ahead
if that's what you want to do.
Give me the matchbox
before you go,
will you ?
I will be out in the courtyard
where no one will mind it
if I smoke.

R. PARTHSARATHY (1934- 2022)

He was born in Tirupparaiturai near Tiruchirapalli, Tamilnadu. He studied in Don Bosco school Siddhartha College, Fort Mumbai and at the University where he was British council scholar. He was a translator, critic,poet and editor.His master piece is *RoughPassage*, a three-part autobiographical poem. He translated the Tamil epic The tale of an Anklet. He was awarded with Ulka Poetry Prize.

23. Exile from Homecoming

My tongue in English chains,
I return, after a generation, to you.
I am at the end
of my dravidic tether,
hunger for you unassuaged.
I falter, stumble.
Speak a tired language
wrenched from its sleep in the Kural,
teeth, palate, lips still new
to its agglutinative touch.
Now, hooked on celluloid, you reel
down plush corridors.
And so it eventually happened—
a family reunion not heard of since grandfather
died in '59 —
in March
this year. Cousins arrived in Tiruchchanur
in overcrowded private buses,
the dust of unlettered years
clouding instant recognition.
Later, each one pulled,
sitting crosslegged on the steps
of the choultry, familiar coconuts out of the fire
of rice-and-pickle afternoons.
Sundari, who had squirrelled up and down
forbidden tamarind trees in her long skirt
every morning with me,
stood there, that day, forty years taller,
her three daughters floating like safe planets near her.

I made myself an expert
in farewells. An unexpected November
shut the door in my face:
I crashed, a glasshouse
hit by the stone of Father's death.
At the burning ghat
relations stood like exclamation points.
The fire stripped his unwary body of the
last shred of family likeness.
I am my father now.
The lines of my hands
hold the fine compass of his going:
I shall follow. And after me,
my unborn son, through the eye of this needle
of forgetfulness.
With paper boats boys tickle her ribs,
and buffaloes have turned her to a pond.
There's eaglewood in her hair
and stale flowers. Every evening,
as bells roll in the forehead of temples,
she sees a man on the steps
clean his arse. Kingfishers and egrets,
whom she fed, have flown
her paps. Also emperors and poets
who slept in her arms. She is become
a sewer, now. No one has any use for Vaikai,
river, once, of this sweet city.
The street in the evening tilts homeward as
traffic piles up. It is then I stir about.
Rise from the table and shake the dust
from my eyes. Pick up
my glasses and look for myself
in every nook and corner

of the night. The pavement turns informer
hearing my steps. A pariah dog
slams an alley in my face.
I have exchanged the world
for a table and chair. I shouldn't complain.
I see him now sitting at his desk.
The door is open. It is evening.
On the lawns the children play.
He went for the wrong gods from the start.
And marriage made it worse.
He hadn't read his Greek poets well:
better to bury a woman than marry her.
Now he teaches. Reviles verse
written by others. Is invited to conferences
and attends them. How long it had taken
him to learn he had no talent at all,
although words came easy.
One can be articulate about nothing.
Or, was it simply his god had left him?
Pedalling his bicycle glasses, he asks,
'What's it like to be a poet?
I say to myself, 'The son of a bitch
fattens himself on the flesh of dead poets.
Lines his pockets with their blood.
From his fingertips ooze ink and paper,
as he squats on the dungheap
of old texts and obscure commentaries.
His eyes peal off.
Where would His Eminence be
but for the poets who splashed about
in the Hellespont or burned in the Java Sea?'
I am no longer myself as I watch the
evening blur the traffic to

a pair of obese headlights.
I returnhome, tired,
my lace pressed against the window
of expectation. I climb the steps
to my flat, only to trip over the mat outside the door.
The key goes to sleep in my palm.
I fear I have bungled again.
That last refinement of speech terrifies me.
The balloon
of poetry has grown red in the face
with repeated blowing. For scriptures I, therefore,
recommend
the humble newspaper: I find
my prayers occasionally answered there.
I shall, perhaps, go on
like this, unmindful of day
melting into the night.
My heart I have turned inside out.
Hereafter, I should be content,
I think, to go through life
with the small change of uncertainties.

KAMALA SURAIYA DAS
(1934-2009)

She was born in Palayamkottai, in Kerala. She was educated in Christian missionary school in Kolkatta and lived in Mumbai after her marriage. She mainly wrote poems and translated some of the Malayalam works into English. She wrote both in English and Malayalam. *My Story* is her most popular autobiography. Her *CollectedPoems*came out in 2000. She died in Pune 2006 and buried in the courtyard of a Mosque in her native. She got the Sahitya Akademi Award for her contribution to Indian English poetry.

24. My Grandmother's House

There is a house now far away where once
I received love... That woman died,
The house withdrew into silence, snakes moved
Among books, I was then too young
To read, and my blood turned cold like the moon
How often I think of going
There, to peer through blind eyes of windows or
Just listen to the frozen air,
Or in wild despair, pick an armful of
Darkness to bring it here to lie
Behind my bedroom door like a brooding
Dog...you cannot believe, darling,
Can you, that I lived in such a house and
Was proud, and loved.... I who have lost
My way and beg now at strangers' doors to
Receive love, at least in small change?

25. Words

All round me are words, and words and words,
They grow on me like leaves, they never
Seem to stop their slow growing
From within... But I tell my self, words
Are a nuisance, beware of them, they
Can be so many things, a
Chasm where running feet must pause, to
Look, a sea with paralyzing waves,
A blast of burning air or,
A knife most willing to cut your best
Friend's throat... Words are a nuisance, but.
They grow on me like leaves ona tree,
They never seem to stop their coming,
From a silence, somewhere deep within...

26. Spoiling the Name

I have a name, had it for thirty
Years, chosen by someone else
For convenience, but when you say
Don't spoil your name, Ifeel I
Must laugh, for I know I have a life
To be lived, and each nameless
Corpuscle in me, has its life to
Be lived... why should this name, so
Sweet-sounding, enter at all the room
Where I go to meet a man
Who gives me nothing but himself, who
Calls me in his private hours
By no name, or the city's dusty
Streets where on afternoons
I walk, looking for old books, antiques,
Way? Why should I remember or bear
That sweet-sounding name, pinned to
Me, a medal, undeservingly
Gained, at moments when, all of
Me is ablaze with life? You ask of
Me a silly thing. Carry
This gift of a name like a corpse and
Totter beneath its weight
And perhaps even fall... I who love
This gift of life more than all I

27. An Introduction

I don't know politics but I know the names
Of those in power, and can repeat them like
Days of week, or names of months, beginning with Nehru.
I amIndian, very brown, born inMalabar,
I speak three languages, write in
Two, dream in one.
Don't write in English, they said, English is
Not your mother-tongue. Why not leave
Me alone, critics, friends, visiting cousins,
Every one of you? Why not let me speak in
Any language I like? The language I speak,
Becomes mine, its distortions, its queernesses
All mine, mine alone.
It is half English, halfIndian, funny perhaps,
but it is honest,
It is as human as I am human, don't
You see? It voices my joys, my longings, my
Hopes, and it is useful to me as cawing
Is to crows or roaring to the lions, it
Is human speech, the speech of the mind that is
Here and not there, a mind that sees and hears and
Is aware. Not the deaf, blind speech
Of trees in storm or of monsoon clouds or of rain or the
Incoherent mutterings of the blazing
Funeral pyre. I was child, and later they
Told me I grew, for I became tall, my limbs
Swelled and one or two places sprouted hair.
WhenI asked for love, not knowing what else to ask
For, he drew a youth of sixteen into the

Bedroom and closed the door, He did not beat me
But my sad woman-body felt so beaten.
The weight of my breasts and womb crushed me.
I shrank Pitifully.
Then … I wore a shirt and my
Brother's trousers, cut my hair short and ignored
My womanliness. Dress in sarees, be girl
Be wife, they said. Be embroiderer, be cook,
Be a quarreller with servants. Fit in. Oh,
Belong, cried the categorizers. Don't sit
On walls or peep in through our lace-draped windows.
Be Amy, or be Kamala. Or, better
Still, be Madhavikutty. It is time to
Choose a name, a role. Don't play pretending games.
Don't play at schizophrenia or be a
Nympho. Don't cry embarrassingly loud when
Jilted in love … I met a man, loved him. Call
Him not by any name, he is every man
Who wants. a woman, just as I am every
Woman who seeks love. In him . . . the hungry haste
Of rivers, in me . . . the oceans' tireless
Waiting. Who are you, I ask each and everyone,
The answer is, it is I. Anywhere and,
Everywhere, I see the one who calls himself I
In this world, he is tightly packed like the
Sword in its sheath. It is I who drink lonely
Drinks at twelve, midnight, in hotels of strange towns,
It is I who laugh, it is I who make love
And then, feel shame, it is I who lie dying
With a rattle in my throat. I am sinner,
I am saint. I am the beloved and the
Betrayed. I have no joys that are not yours, no
Aches which are not yours. I too call myself I.

28. Someone Else's Song

I am a million, million people
Talking all at once, with voices
Raised in clamour, like maids
At village-wells.
I am a million, million deaths
Pox-clustered, each a drying seed
Someday to be shed, to grow for
Someone else, a memory.
I am a million, million births
Flushed with triumphant blood, each a growing
Thing that thrusts its long-nailed hands
To scar the hollow air.

SYED AMMANUDDIN(1934-)

He was born in Mysore and had his under graduation and post-graduation in India and later he obtained his doctorate of philosophy in United States of America. His books are- *ChallengerPoems*, *The Children of Hiroshima Poems*, Adventures of Atman, An Epic of the Soul. He was poet with the blend of Indian essence and American flavour in his writings. He translated some of his poems in French and Urdu and Kannada.

29. Don't Call Me Indo-Anglian

no I don't want to be
a hotchpotch of culture
a confusion of language
a nullity of imagination
an abortive affair between an Indo and an Anglo
I hate hyphens
the artificial bridges
between artificial values
in the name of race religion n language
I damn all hyphenated minds prejudiced
Off-springs of unenlightened souls
I denounce all labels and labelmakers
I refuse to be a moonrock
specimen to be analyzed labelled n stored
for a curious gloomy fellow to reanalyze
reclassify me for shelving me again
they call me indo-anglian
I don't know what they mean cauvery
flows in my veins chamundi hills rise
in my mind with stars a float eyes of the
goddess smiling on the slain demonbrindavan
fountains sing in my soul but
I am not tied down to my childhood scene.
I have led languages by their ears
I have twisted creeds to force the truth out
I have burned candles in the caves of prejudice
I have surged in the oceans of being
I have flown across the universe on the wings of my thought
they call me indo-anglian the mistaken misinformed

folk n class me with a small group of
writers cloistering me crippling me
I would rather roam with Kalidasa n Kabir or
go on a spiritual journey with dante
meditate with Khayyam on the mathematics
of existence or sing with Ghalib
the anguish of love or drown with
li po kissing the moon's reflection in the river they
call me indo-anglianit's true
I write in English dream in the language of Shakespeare n
Keats but I am not an Anglo my friend
I am a POET
I have lived forty centuries under various names
I am now Amanuddin

EKI. N.DARUWALLA (1937-)

He was born in Lahore in 1937. He was an Indian poet and short story writer in English, He was also a former Indian Police Service officer. He was awarded the Sahitya Akademi award in 1984 for his contribution to Indian English poetry. *The Keeper of the Dead* is is the most remembered collection of poems. Also he was awarded with the Padmashri. His other works are- *WinterPoems, UnderOrion, Apparition in April* and *CollectedPoems*(1970).

30. Pestilence in Nineteenth – Century Calcutta

'said the sahib's barber to him
referring to the ghettoes
beyond the esplanade
where people writhed
in the groaning callisthenics of cholera.
Bacteria and bacillus throve in the wells,
nestled under the spawn-beds
and killed. The fires burnt higher,
and the dead went up
like fragments of liturgies
lost in a great wind
The sahib was shocked. This had never struck him.
In this land of mud and mire,
death was everywhere:
the water was heavy with it
like a woman with child,
and you could pick it up from the earth
as you pick up fallen fruit.
But it was the sahibs
who fell like skittles, the Reinharts
De Bussys, Claude Martins,
the Smiths and the Lawrences,
British and French and Dutch,
interred in the same loam,
mourned by the same tolling bells
their remains bristling with like crucifixes.
The climate killed: not .so much

the summer sun which spiked them
through their sola topis,
but those vaporous exhalations
of the earth after the rains
which brought on the fevers and the fluxes.
And always it was so sudden.
You lunched with a fellow and by dusk
he was dead, and the tolling from the belfry
was the only way you heard of it.
It was the whites who carried
this fear of death like a slipped disc through their lives
and paid the surgeon one gold mohur
for a visit, one rupee for an ounce of salts,
two for an ounce of bark, paid him
for blood-letting, for being cupped and leeched
and blistered with hot irons
and fed on opium and mercurous chloride.
Twelve years with the John Company
and he had never thought of death
hacking away with its scythe
as it swung past the black ghettoes,
where the native spawn petrified
almost before it left the womb.
And then hardly ten days after
the barber had spoken,
he went down the Hooghly
on his winter tour where his Sikh abdar
who had served him during
the bara hazri, fell stricken. The next day
our man Friday told him, 'Now disease
come to stomach sahib, now
story finish.' In dysentery
a gut feeling ceases to be

premonitory. That evening the Kanjars*
burnt him, guts and all.
The funeral expenses would be his
he said, choking a little, and
ashamed of the tears he held back.
The bill presented on a tray next morning
made him blink. It read,
'Five rupees for roasted Sardar.'

DOM MORAES (1938-2004)

Born in Mumbai, he studied in Jesus College, Oxford, England. His father Franck Moraes, was a celebrate author and journalist worked with many news papers, including Indian Express. He Dom became an Indian writer and a poet published nearly 30 collections of poems in English. He was widely seen as foundational figure in Indian English poetic tradition. His poems are meaningful and his poetry is substantial contribution to Indian English Literature. *A Beginning* (1958), *Poems*(1960) and *JohnNobody*(1965) are his main poetical works. He won Hawthorndoen Prize in 1958 and Sahitya Akademi award in 1994.

31. A Letter

Almost I can recall where I was born;
The hot verandas where the chauffeurs drowse
Backyard dominion of the ragged thorn,
And nameless servants in my father's house,
Whispering together in the backyard dirt
Until their talk came true for me one day:
My father hugging me so hard it hurt,
My mother mad, and time we went away.
We travelled and I looked for love too young.
More travel, and I looked for lust instead.
I was not ruled by wanting: I was young,
And poems grew like maggots in my head.
A fighting South-East Asia, with each gun
Talking to me, then homeward to the green
And dung- smeared plains ruled over by the sun.
When I had done with that, I was fifteen.
At sixteen I came here to start again
I stumbled dumbly through the English rain,
The literature, the drink, the talk, talk, talk.
I wrote about them: It was waste of breath.
For many they were home, for me too wild,
Too walled for me those valleys full of death
Who had grown up as wanderer and child.
Of one dying poet I was not afraid,
In conversation like an avalanche,
Convincing mainly by the noise he made.
He reinforced his views with gin-and-French.
Wrinkled and heaving, tuskless elephant,
He levelled a thick finger, grained with ink.

one more drink. Three winters I was drunk:
one early spring Brought me first love for you,
my great good news;
Then my excuse to play the drunken king,
Staggering through bars, became a bad excuse.
The naked valleys shaken with alarms
Where hawk and serpent watched,
were touched, and slept. Morning
and night your image in my arms
Taught me a harder task than to accept.
Earlier in time I prayed to be forgiven.
Through tide-scurf to the acreage of the whale,
Truest to loneliness my sail was driven.
I have forgotten, making landfall where
Chin in your hand, you sit and gentle things
Drift on your dream, transparent river where
The swan sleeps with her young under her wings.

GOPAL HONNALEGERE
(1942-2003)

He was born in Bijapur, Karnataka in 1942 and had his early education(school and college) in Mysore. K.A,Jayaseelan edited his *CollectedPoems.*His poetry had different poetic style than those of Mumbai school. His works are- *A Wad of Poems, A Gesture of Fleshless Sound,* and *Intermodes.*

32. Grass Words

Men stay in air-conditioned rooms
Men work getting blisters in the sun
I am a sunflower
Working coolly I get no sun-stroke.
Earthquake crumbles leading banks
Flood dissolves the Parliament
I am an earth worm
I am secure beneath the earth.
Storm blows away the neon signs of advertisement
Time fades away the mirage nimbus of prophets
I am glow-worm
None can take away my glow.
State Gambles with men
Men gable with the state,
I am grass
Let me live and work,
My goddness
The meadows are green
My horse may win some day.

33. Of Crows

I

My grandpa used to say
The old man
among *the*crow tribe whose digestion
was dull whose eye-sight was falling short
who spent very little time in hunting ran a school
on the outskirts of the city
near a temple tank
on an old banyan tree
in the early hours of morning
in the true public school
tradition to teach the crow chicks
how to caw in 24 different tones
in such a school
naturally/grandpa said
the koel chicks
who could never caw
go! the battering corporal punishment
but they soon learnt
to fly and flew away
like the nomad aryans
vedic hymns
flew away from
the brahmins' tongue
at the dawn of english
and british raj
but the story does not end here grandpa
continued here and there one or two crow
chicks started believing that they too are koels

and tried to sing like kocto they too created
a hindu metaphysics but all in alienation
II
when ramu uncle kept
four yellow rice balls in the
backyard and waited to see the
old man's soul coming in a crow
to eat them on grandpa's first death
anniversary the crows
which used to trouble grandma
so much every day
even sometimes entering her kitchen
did not turn up at all
till 12 o'clock
"nowadays
bangalore is full of mice and bandicoots
which are very nutritious
no crow is foolish enough
to fill half its stomach
with your brahmin's polished rice"
said one of my uncles
who was a doctor
the crows did not turn up
even at 3 o'clock
I said to ramu uncle
"your priest is very proud, he has
read the four tragedies of Shakespeare
like four vedas in his b.a. (hons).
he says nowadays nobody reads
Shakespeare in original, even the
m.a. students read bazaar notes,
he has even read max mueller and
the golden bough, he can talk so

much and so well on upanishads.
it seems, he wanted to become a
philosophy lecturer but his father
forced him to continue the family
profession, but he is happy, he says,
he can earn as a priest
more than what a lecturer can. he can easily become a
god-man in america but he is very much sentimentally
attached to his wife and children, he speaks good
english but chants all the vedic hymns with a strong
english intonation, why don't you ask him to bring a
crow in a cage, next time? it will be fun to see
grandpa's soul in priesf s crow in a priest's cage!
does it sound surrealistic?
but if he brings, it will be a surrealistic ritual,
Andre breton's soul will come to see it!"
we joked, we laughed and talked
none of us felt hungry
we had a very heavy breakfast
the crows did not turn up even at 4 O'clock
grandma could not bear to see her elder son waiting
she said "Ramu your father was a good man.
I think he has attained moksha. his soul
has become one with god. it does not return
to see us. go and have your food".
we laughed and went to have our food.
we knew very well
that grandma did not love grandpa.

34. The Donkeys

May be it's in a legend
I don't remember his name a
Tibetan poet sat and wrote
poems poems poems
all his life when he was
eighty-nine and with a
mirror-like bald head
approaching death
he had with him three
donkey-loads of poems
he wanted to give them away
to a prayer wheel-turning monastery
he carried them on three hired donkeys
and began to walk thinking about life
it was a god-freezing winter
the old man started shivering
and couldn't walk
he made a bonfire of
one of his donkey-loads of poems
and warmed himself sitting near
the fire when he was about
to start on the journey a thought
came into his mind he saw the donkeys,
recalling one of his poems on donkeys,
the donkeys too were shivering he
again made a bonfire of his two
remaining donkey-loads and made
the donkeys stand around the
fire in trinity the critics say

a single unburnt line of his poetry
discovered by posterity is enough
to express all his perception you
search for the donkey you ride on

AUSTRALIA

A.B.PATERSON (1864-1941)

Andrew Barton "Banjo" Paterson, CBE was an Australian bush poet, journalist, and author. He was also called Banjo Paterson. He wrote many ballads and poems about Australian life, focusing particularly on the rural and outback areas, including the district around Binalong, New South Wales, where he spent much of his childhood.

35. Waltzing Matilda

Once a jolly swagman camped by a billabong
Under the shade of a Coolibah tree;
And he sang as he looked at the old billy boiling
"Who'll come a-waltzing Matilda with me."
Chorus Waltzing Matilda, Waltzing Matildam,
Who'll come a-waltzing Matilda, my darling.
Who'll come a-waltzing Matilda with me.
Waltzing Matilda and leading a water-bag.
Who'll come a-waltzing Matilda with me.
Down came a jumbuck to drink at that billagong,
Up came the jumbuck to drink at the waterhole,
Up jumped the swagman and grabbed him with glee;
And he sang as he put him away in his tucker-bag,
"Who'll come a-waltzing Matilda with me."
Chorus Waltzing Matilda, Waltzing Matilda
Who'll come a-waltzing Matilda, my darling.
Who'll come a-waltzing Matilda with me.
Waltzing Matilda and leading a water-bag.
Who'll come a-waltzing Matilda with me.
Up came the squatter a-riding his thoroughbred;
Up came the policeman - one, two, and three.
"Whose is the jumbuck you've got in the tucker-bag?
You'll come a-waltzing Matilda with we."
Chorus Waltzing matilda, Waltzing Matilda
You'll come a-waltzing Matilda, my darling.
You'll come a-waltzing Matilda with me.
Waltzing Matilda and leading a water-bag.
You'll come a-waltzing Matilda with me.
Up jumped the swagman and sprang into the billabong,

"You'll never catch me alive!" said he
And his ghost may be heard as you pass by that billabong,
You'll come a-waltzing Matilda with me!"
"Chorus Waltzing Matilda, Waltzing Matilda,
You'll come a –Waltzing Matilda with me!
And his ghost may be heard as you pass by that
Billabong,
"You'll come a-waltzing Matilda with me!"

SHAW NEILSON (1872-1942)

He was an Australian poet . slightly built for the most of his life, he worked as a labourer fruit-picking , clearing scrub, navvying and working in quarries , and after 1928 he began working as a messenger with the Country Roads Broad in Melborune. Hismainworks are-
HeartofSpring(1919), *Ballads andLyricalPoems*,(1923)
BeautyImposesSomeRecentVerse (1938) *Unpublished Poems*,(1947).

36. To a Blue Flower

I would be dismal with all the fine pearls of
the crown of a king;
But I can talk plainly to you, you little blue
flower of the Spring!
Here in the heart of September the world that
I walk in is full
Of the hot happy sound of the shearing, the
rude heavy scent of the wool.
Soon would I tire of all riches or honours or
power that they fling;
But you are my own, of my own folk, you little
blue flower of the Spring!
I was around by the cherries to-day; all the
cherries are pale:
The world is a woman in velvet: the air is the
colour of ale.
I would be dismal with all the fine pearls of the
crown of a king;
But I can give love-talk to you, you little blue
flower of the Spring!

37. Surely God was a Lover

Surely God was a lover when He bade the day begin
Soft as a woman's eyelid — white as a woman's skin.
Surely God was a lover, with a lover's faults and fears,
When He made the sea as bitter as a wilful woman's tears.
Surely God was a lover, with the madness love will bring:
He wrought while His love was singing, and put her
soul in the Spring.
Surely God was a lover, by a woman's wile controlled,
When He made the Summer a woman thirsty
and unconsoled.
Surely God was a lover when He made the trees so fair:
In every leaf is a glory caught from a woman's hair.
Surely God was a lover — see, in the flowers He grows,
His love's eyes in the violet — her sweetness in the rose.

38. Stony Town

If ever I go to Stony Town, I'll go as to a fair,
With bells and men and a dance-girl with the
heat-wave in her hair:
I'll ask the birds that live on the road; for I dream
(though it may not be)
That the eldest song was a forest thought and the
singer was a tree.
Oh, Stony Town is a hard town! It buys and
sells and buys:
It will not pity the plights of youth or any love
in the eyes:
No curve they follow in Stony Town; but the
straight line and the square:
—And the girl shall dance them a royal dance,
like a blue wren at his prayer.
Oh, Stony Town is a hard town! It sells and
buys and sells:
—Merry men three I will take with me, and
seven and twenty bells:
The bells will laugh and the men will laugh,
and the girl shall shine so fair
With the scent of love and cinnamon dust shaken
out of her hair.
Her skirts shall be of the gossamer, full thirty inches high;
And her lips shall move as the flowers move to
see the winds go by:
The men will laugh, and the bells will laugh, to
find the world so young;
And the girl shall go as a velvet bird, with a

quick step on her tongue.
She shall cry aloud that a million moons for a lover
is not long,
And her mouth shall be as the green honey in
the honey-eater's song:
—If ever I go to Stony Town, I'll go as to a fair,
And the girl shall shake with the cinnamon and
the heat-wave in her hair.

39. The Bard and the Lizard

The lizard leans in to October,
He walks on the yellow and green,
The world is awake and unsober,
It knows where the lovers have been:
The wind, like a violoncello,
Comes up and commands him to sing:
He says to me, "Courage, good fellow!
We live by the folly of Spring!"
A fish that the sea cannot swallow,
A bird that can never yet rise,
A dreamer no dreamer can follow,
The snake is at home in his eyes.
He tells me the paramount treason,
His words have the resolute ring:
"Away with the homage to Reason!
We live by the folly of Spring!"
The leaves are about him; the berry
Is close in the red and the green,
His eyes are too old to be merry,
He knows where the lovers have been.
And yet he could never be bitter,
He tells me no sorrowful thing:
"The Autumn is less than a twitter!
We live by the folly of Spring!"
As green as the light on a salad
He leans in the shade of a tree,
He has the good breath of a ballad,
The strength that is down in the sea.
How silent he creeps in the yellow —

How silent! and yet can he sing:
He gives me, "Good morning, good fellow!
We live by the folly of Spring!"
I scent the alarm of the faded
Who love not the light and the play,
I hear the assault of the jaded,
I hear the intolerant bray.
My friend has the face of a wizard,
He tells me no desolate thing:
I learn from the heart of the lizard,
We live by the folly of Spring!

KENNETH SLESSOR (1901-1971)

Kenneth Adolphe Slessor OBE was an Australian poet, journalist and official war correspondent during World War II. He was born in Orange, a city in the east -central New South Wales.Australia. He studied in Mowbray High School and Sidney Church of English grammar He was one of the Australia's leading poets,, notable particularly for the absorption of modernist influences into Australian poetry. A poetry awards as named after him. His main works are- Beach *Burial*, Earth Visitors, *The Bells* etc.

40. Country Towns

Country towns, with your willows and squares,
And farmers bouncing on barrel mares
To public houses of yellow wood
With "1860" over their doors,
And that mysterious race of Hogans
Which always keeps the General Stores....
At the School of Arts, a broadsheet lies
Sprayed with the sarcasm of flies:
"The Great Go lightly Family
Of Entertainers Here To-night"–
Dated a year and a half ago,
But left there, less from carelessness
Than from a wish to seem polite.
Verandas baked with musky sleep,
Mulberry faces dozing deep,
And dogs that lick the sunlight up
Like paste of gold – or, roused in vain
By far, mysterious buggy-wheels,
Lower their ears, and drowse again...
Country towns with your schooner bees,
And locusts burnt in the pepper-trees,
Drown me with syrups, arch your boughs,
Find me a bench, and let me snore,
Till, charged with ale and unconcern,
I'll think it's noon at half-past four!

41. Beach Burial

Softly and humbly to the Gulf of Arabs
The convoys of dead sailors come;
At night they sway and wander in the waters far under,
But morning rolls them in the foam.
Between the sob and clubbing of the gunfire
Someone, it seems, has time for this,
To pluck them from the shallows and bury
them in burrows
And tread the sand upon their nakedness;
And each cross, the driven stake of tidewood,
Bears the last signature of men,
Written with such perplexity, with such bewildered pity,
The words choke as they begin –
'*Unknownseaman*' – the ghostly pencil
Wavers and fades, the purple drips,
The breath of the wet season has washed their inscriptions
As blue as drowned men's lips,
Dead seamen, gone in search of the same landfall,
Whether as enemies they fought,
Or fought with us, or neither; the sand
joins them together,
Enlisted on the other front.

A. D. HOPE (1907-2000)

Alec Derwent Hope AC OBE was an Australian poet and essayist known for his satirical slant in poetry. He was born in Cooma, New South Wales. He was also a critic, teacher and academic. He was referred to the in an American journal as 'the 20th century's greatest 18th century poet.". His main works are - *The Wandering Islands, Poems, Collected Poems, 1930-1965*, and *A Book of Answers*. He was awarded with FAW Christopher Brennan Award for poetry.

42. Australia

A nation of trees, drab green and desolate grey
In the field uniform of modern wars
Darkens her hills, those endless, outstretched paws
Of Sphinx demolished or stone lion worn away.
They call her a young country, but they lie:
She is the last of lands, the emptiest,
A woman beyond her change of life, a breast
Still tender but within the womb is dry.
Without songs, architecture, history:
The emotions and superstitions of younger lands,
Her rivers of water drown among inland sands,
The river of her immense stupidity
Floods her monotonous tribes from Cairns to Perth.
In them at last the ultimate men arrive
Whose boast is not: 'we live' but 'we survive',
A type who will inhabit the dying earth.
And her five cities, like five teeming sores,
Each drains her: a vast parasite robber-state
Where second-hand Europeans pullulate
Timidly on the edge of alien shores.
Yet there are some like me turn gladly home
From the lush jungle of modern thought, to find
The Arabian desert of the human mind,
Hoping, if still from the deserts the prophets come,
Such savage and scarlet as no green hills dare
Springs in that waste, some spirit which escapes
The learned doubt, the chatter of cultured apes
Which is called civilization over there.

43. Standardization

A Nation of trees, drab green and desolate grey
In the field uniform of modern wars,
Darkens her hills, those endless, outstretched paws
Of Sphinx demolished or stone lion worn away.
They call her a young country, but they lie:
She is the last of lands, the emptiest,
A woman beyond her change of life, a breast
Still tender but within the womb is dry.
Without songs, architecture, history:
The emotions and superstitions of younger lands,
Her rivers of water drown among inland sands,
The river of her immense stupidity
Floods her monotonous tribes from Cairns to Perth.
In them at last the ultimate men arrive
Whose boast is not: "we live" but "we survive",
A type who will inhabit the dying earth.
And her five cities, like five teeming sores,
Each drains her: a vast parasite robber-state
Where second hand Europeans pullulate
Timidly on the edge of alien shores.
Yet there are some like me turn gladly home
From the lush jungle of modern thought, to find
The Arabian desert of the human mind,
Hoping, if still from the deserts the prophets come,
Such savage and scarlet as no green hills dare
Springs in that waste, some spirit which escapes
The learned doubt, the chatter of cultured apes
Which is called civilization over there.

44. The Death of the Bird

For every bird there is this last migration:
Once more the cooling year kindles her heart;
With a warm passage to the summer station
Love pricks the course in lights across the chart.
Year after year a speck on the map, divided
By a whole hemisphere, summons her to come;
Season after season, sure and safely guided,
Going away she is also coming home.
And being home, memory becomes a passion
With which she feeds her brood and straws her nest,
Aware of ghosts that haunt the heart's possession
And exiled love mourning within the breast.
The sands are green with a mirage of valleys;
The palm-tree casts a shadow not its own;
Down the long architrave of temple or palace
Blows a cool air from moorland scarps of stone.
And day by day the whisper of love grows stronger;
That delicate voice, more urgent with despair,
Custom and fear constraining her no longer,
Drives her at last on the waste leagues of air.
A vanishing speck in those inane dominions,
Single and frail, uncertain of her place,
Alone in the bright host of her companions,
Lost in the blue unfriendliness of space,
She feels it close now, the appointed season:
The invisible thread is broken as she flies;
Suddenly, without warning, without reason,
The guiding spark of instinct winks and dies.
Try as she will, the trackless world delivers

No way, the wilderness of light no sign,
The immense and complex map of hills and rivers
Mocks her small wisdom with its vast design.
And darkness rises from the eastern valleys,
And the winds buffet her with their hungry breath,
And the great earth, with neither grief nor malice,
Receives the tiny burden of her death.

45. Moschus Moschiferus A Song for St. Cecilia's Day

In the high jungle where Assam meets Tibet
The small Kastura, most archaic of deer,
Were driven in herds to cram the hunters' net
And slaughtered for the musk-pods which they bear;
But in those thickets of rhododendron and birch
The tiny creatures now grow hard to find.
Fewer and fewer survive each year. The search
Employs new means, more exquisite and refined:
The hunters now set out by two or three;
Each carries a bow and one a slender flute.
Deep in the forest the archers choose a tree
And climb; the piper squats against the root.
And there they wait until all trace of man
And rumour of his passage dies away.
They melt into the leaves and, while they scan
The glade below, their comrade starts to play.
Through those vast listening woods a tremulous skein
Of melody wavers, delicate and shrill:
Now dancing and now pensive, now a rain
Of pure bright drops of sound, and now the still,
Sad wailing of lament; from tune to tune
It winds and modulates without a pause;
The hunters hold their breath; the trace of noon
Grows tense; with its full power the music draws
A shadow from a juniper's darker shade;
Bright-eyed, with quivering muscle and pricked ear,
The little musk deer slips into the glade

Led by an ecstacy that conquers fear.
A wild enchantment lures him, step by step,
Into its net of crystalline sound until
The leaves stir overhead, the bowstrings snap
And poisoned shafts bite sharp into the kill.
Then, as the victim shudders, leaps and falls,
The music soars to a delicious peak,
And on and on its silvery piping calls
Fresh spoil for the rewards the hunters seek.
But when the woods are emptied and the dusk
Draws in, the men climb down and count their prey,
Cut out the little glands that hold the musk
And leave the carcasses to rot away.
A hundred thousand or so are killed each year;
Cause and effect are very simply linked:
Rich scents demand the musk, and so the deer,
Its source, must soon, they say, become extinct.
Divine Cecilia, there is no more to say!
Of all who praised the power of music, few
Knew of these things. In honour of your day
Accept this song I too have made for you.

JUDITH WRIGHT (1915-2000)

Judith Arundell Wright was born in Armidale, in New South Wales. She was poet, critic, and short story writer. She was married to Jack McKinney was an Australian poetess, environmentalist,and campaigner for Aboriginal land rights. She published more than 50 books. Her main works are- *Moving Image*(1946) *Woman to Man* (1949) *CollectedPoems*(1949-1971) *The Human Pattern*(1990) and *The Cry for the Dead* (1981). She was a recipient of the Christopher Brennan Award for poetry.

46. Woman to Man

The eyeless labourer in the night,
the selfless, shapeless seed I hold,
builds for its resurrection day —
silent and swift and deep from sight
foresees the unimagined light.
This is no child with a child's face;
this has no name to name it by:
yet you and I have known it well.
This is our hunter and our chase,
the third who lay in our embrace.
This is the strength that your arm knows,
the arc of flesh that is my breast,
the precise crystals of our eyes.
This is the blood's wild tree that grows
the intricate and folded rose.
This is the maker and the made;
this is the question and reply;
the blind head butting at the dark,
the blaze of light along the blade.
Oh hold me, for I am afraid.

47. Typists in the Phoenix Building

In tiled and fireproof corridors
the typists shelter in their sex;
perking beside the half-cock clerks,
they set a curl on freckled necks.
The formal bird above the doors
Is set in metal whorls of flame.
The train goes aching on its rails.
Its rising cry of steel and wheels
intolerably comes, and falls
on walls immaculate and dumb.
Comptrollers and calculators
compute the frequency of fires,
adduce the risk, add up the years.
Drawn by late-afternoon desires
The poles of mind meet lust's equators.
Where will the inundation reach
whose cycle we can but await?
The city burns in summer heat
grass withers and the season's late;
the metal bird would scorch the touch;
and yet above some distant source,
some shrunken lake or spring gone dry,
perhaps the clouds involve the day in night,
and once again on high the blazing sun forgets its course.
deep-hidden in that whirling smoke
from which the floods of Nile may fall.
But summer burns the city still.
The metal bird upon the wall
Is silent; Shirley and her clerk

in tiled and fireproof corridors
touch and fall apart. No fires
consume the banked comptrollers;
no flood has lipped the inlaid floors.

48. The Harp and the King

Old king without a throne,
the hollow of despair
behind his obstinate unyielding stare,
knows only, God is gone:
and, fingers clenching on his chair,
feels night and the soul's terror coming on.
Bring me that harp, that singer, Let him sing.
Let something fill the space inside the mind,
that's a dry stream-bed for the flood of fear.
Song's only sound; but it's a lovely sound,
a fountain through the drought.
Bring David here, said the old frightened king.
Sing something. Comfort me.
Make me believe the meaning in the rhyme.
The world's a traitor to the self-betrayed;
but once I thought there was a truth in time,
while now my terror is eternity.
So do not take me outside time.
Make me believe in my mortality,
since that is all I have, the old king said.
I sing the praise of time, the harp replied:
the time of aching drought when the black plain
cannot believe in roots or leaves or rain.
Then lips crack open in the stone-hard peaks;
and rock begins to suffer and to pray when
all that lives has died and withered in the
wind and blown away; and earth has no more
strength to bleed.
I sing the praise of time and of the rain—

the word creation speaks.
Four elements are locked in time;
the sign that makes them fertile is the seed,
and this outlasts all death and springs again,
the running' water of the harp-notes cried.
But the old king sighed obstinately,
How can that comfort me?
Night and the terror of the soul come on,
and out of me both water and seed have gone.
What other generations shall I see?
But make me trust my failure and my fall,
said the sad king, since these are now my all.
I sing the praise of time, the harp replied.
In time we fail, alone with hours and tears,
ruin our followers and traduce our cause,
and give our love its last and fatal hurt.
In time we fail and fall.
In time the company even of God withdraws
and we are left with our own murderous heart.
Yet it is time that holds,
somewhere although not now,
the peal of trumpets for us; time that bears,
made fertile even by those tears,
even by this darkness, even by this loss,
incredible redemptions—hours that grow,
as trees grow fruit, in a blind holiness,
the truths unknown, the loves unloved by us.
But the old king turned his head sullenly.
How can that comfort me,
who see into the heart as deep as God can see?
Love's sown in us; perhaps it flowers; it dies.
I failed my God and I betrayed my love.
Make me believe in treason; that is all I have.

This is the praise of time, the harp cried out—
that we betray all truths that we possess.
Time strips the soul and leaves it comfortless
and sends it thirsty through a bone-white drought.
Time's subtler treacheries teach us to betray.
What else could drive us on our way?
Wounded we cross the desert's emptiness,
and must be false to what would make us whole.
For only change and distance shape for us
some new tremendous symbol for the soul.

49. Clock and Heart

The trap of time surprised my heart—
its hidden teeth of circumstance
that draw the child into the clock
upon the cogs of tick and tock. No logic,
artifice nor chance could
silence my protesting heart.
Then poetry's electing shade
enclosed me with its darkening ray,
left me no face to recognize,
no eyes to meet my search eyes.
The solitude of poetry
locked me within its second shade.
To light that shade and set me free
no flame had power but human love.
Against my will I caught and burned,
but then the key of time was turned,
the dark ray blazed, and from above
it lit the hour that set me free.
Set free at last in human time—
that long-rejected tyranny—
I found in ordinary love
the solitudes of poetry.

50. Nigger's Leap, New England

The eastward spurs tip backward from the sun,
Night runs an obscure tide round cape and bay
and beats with boats of cloud up from the sea
against this sheer and limelit granite head.
Swallow the spine of range; be dark, O lonely air.
Make a cold quilt across the bone and skull
that screamed falling in flesh from the lipped cliff
and then were silent, waiting for the flies.
Here is the symbol, and the climbing dark
a time for synthesis. Night buoys no warning
over the rocks that wait our keels; no bells
sound for her mariners. Now must we measure
our days by nights, our tropics by their poles,
love by its end and all our speech by silence.
See in these gulfs, how small the light of home.
Did we not know their blood channelled our rivers,
and the black dust our crops ate was their dust?
O all men are one man at last. We should have known
the night that tided up the cliffs and hid them
had the same question on its tongue for us.
And there they lie that were ourselves writ strange.
Never from earth again the coolant
or thin black children dancing like the shadows
of saplings in the wind. Night lips the harsh
scarp of the table land and cools its granite.
Night floods us suddenly as history
that has sunk many islands in its good time.

JAMES MC AULEY(1917-1976)

James Phillip McAuley was born in Lakemaba, Australia. He studied in Fort Street High school and University of Sidney. He was an Australian academic, poet journalist literary critic prominent convert to Roman Catholicism. He was involved in the Ern Malley Poetry hoax. His works are- *CollectedPoems, Versification: A Short introduction, A Map of Australian Verse.*

51. From the True Discovery of Australia

The place, my lord, is much like Gideon's fleece
The second time he laid it on the ground;
For by the will of God it has remained
Bone-dry itself, with water all around.
Yet, as a wheel that's driven in the ruts,
It has a wet rim where the people clot
Like mud : and though they praise the inner spaces,
When asked to go themselves, they'd rather not.
The men are brave, contentious, ignorant;
The women very much as one expects.
For their religion, I must be excused,
Having no stomach to observe their sects.
You must be wary in your conversation;
For, seeing them thumb-high, you might suppose
They recognized their stature, but beware!
Their notion of themselves is grandiose.
And you will often find, although their heads
Are like a berry on a twig of bones,
They speak as Giants of the South Pacific
And treat the islands as their stepping-stones.
North-east across the water, Brobdingnag
Casts its momentous shadow on the sea
And fills the sky with thunder; but they smile
And sit on their verandas taking tea,
Watching through the pleasant afternoons
Flood fire and cyclone in successive motion
Complete the work the pioneers began

of shifting all the soil into the ocean.
Sometimes they have to light the lamps at noon,
And seal their houses that are shipping dust
Like vessels in a storm; and truth to say
It is a kind of shipwreck. But they trust
In providence: the Almighty's not their own.
Meanwhile, as you'd expect, their arts are poor
As if the dust had leaked into their brains
dry-rot at the core.

52. Invocation

Radiant Muse, my childhood's nurse,
Who gave my wondering mouth to taste
The fragrant honeycomb of verse;
And later smilingly embraced
My boyhood, ripening its crude
Harsh vigour in your solitude:
Compose the mingling thoughts that crowd
Upon me to a lucid line;
Teach me at last to speak aloud
In words that are no longer mine;
For at your touch, discreet, profound,
Ten thousand years softly resound.
I do not now revolt, or quarrel
With the paths you make me tread,
But choose the honeycomb and laurel
And walk with patience towards the dead;
Expecting, where my rest is stayed,
A welcome in that windless shade.
Take salt upon your tongue.
And do not feed the heart
With sorrow, darkness or lies;
These are the death of art
Living is thirst for joy;
That is what art rehearses.
Let sober drunkenness give
Its splendor to your verses.
Move like the sable swan
On the Luminous expanse,
In sight out of range

Of barking ignorance.

VINCENT BUCKLEY(1925-1989)

Vincent Thomas Buckley was Australalin poet, teacher, editor ,essayist and critic. He was born n Romsey, Victoria. He studied in St.Catherine College, St Patrick College, East Melborurne. His main works are *Collected Poems, Henry Handel Richardson* (1961) *LastPoems, Essays in Poetry* (1957),and *MastersinIsrael*(1961). His poems were published in other European languages. A poetry prize was named after him.

53. Late Tutorial

The afternoon dark increases with the clock
And shadows greening on the cabinet.
Teacher of youth, and more than half a fool,
How should you catch those shadows in your net?
Outside, the world's late colour calls us home:
Not to the refuge of familiar art
Nor house of setting wood, but to the first
Home, to the savage entry of the heart.
There, where the dry lips are cooled with words
And every hand worships the love it serves,
Perhaps we'll find some comfort: the deep spring
Rising, and soft renewal of the nerves.
In poetry with its constant singing mouth.
Open the door, then; numbed with winter air,
They smile, and move inside; the colours fade
Ringing my head; they seat themselves, and stare.
So I must learn that these, the learners come
To teach me something of my destiny;
That love's not pity, words are not mine alone,
And all are twinned on the great central tree.
How shall I answer them, give ultimate name
To the nerves at war, the mind in dishabille?
Better to pace with the slow clock, and teach them
Quibbles with which to meet adversity.
Their thoughts come, slow, from a cold bed. Their needs
Are close to me as the smell of my own flesh.
Their timid guesses grow, soft-fallen seeds,
To grace my mind with pain. And should I say
'O man is sick, and suffering from the world,

And I must go to him, my poetry
Lighting his image as a ring of fire,
The terrible and only means I have;
And yet I give too much in rhetoric
What should be moulded with a lifetime's care,
What peace alone should strike, and hear vibrate
To the secret slow contraction of the air'.
The talk would die in loud embarrassment,
The books be rustled and the noses blown
In frenzy of amazement at this short
Still youthful puppet in academic gown.
I cannot, but speak measured foolish words:
Shelley was fitful, Keats a dozing fire.
Pass with the light, poor comrades. You and I
Follow but feebly where our words aspire.

54. Burning the effects

By the chill winds to home. O cherry tree,
Cold flesh, cold stone, cold branch, and dripping leaves
Stand near the house that could not fathom me
Or hold him, the earth your damp earth retrieves.
Mostly, I light a backyard fire to burn
the poor hoardings; a whole lumber-room,
Heaved out of doors, struggles to return
Some showing for a life's delirium;
Flakes whirl like gusts of breath or late desire
Upward; I learn in the new heat of air
How much seeks out its element in fire,
How much too, mocks its own weaknesses there.
A mouse or lone rat scuttles in the wall
Where once, as indestructible, the bees
Swarmed with a sound like burning. Still and all,
Things get cleared away, and a cold breeze
Winnows the sparks enough to make a shine.
Of the black air against the cherry tree.
Nothing of it is absolutely mine,
And he who hoarded it owned nothing. Free.

55. Fellow Traveller

Give him this day his bread of indignation,
For he is Inspector of our Consciences;
Give him his daily signature
To a joint letter; hear him explain,
Oh no, it's not the case itself so much,
It's the principle;
And listen, with half an ear, to hear
Behind the almost empty pipe,
The almost empty eyes,
The high blast of a revolver shot.

56. Youth Leader

In the wedge head the eyes are
Too globally moved, under hair combed forward
In the Roman fashion.
A programme in a hair style.
His torso holds the promise of a paunch.
He is big with history
And the streets go crazy at his lifted hand.
How many dead will bloat the gutters
When he learns to lower it.

57. Parents

My father asks me how I stand it all,
The work, the debts, the spite. My mother talks
As though I were a famous man and yet
Unguarded somehow, too fragile to touch.
It's their needs, not mine, that flutter here
In the questions and the anecdotes. I stare
At the rust encroaching on the walnut-branches
Or the pile of litter where the biggest pine-tree
Used to stand, before my absence killed it.
Their door has a vine over it; they murmur
Endearments to the animals, and cry
At small wrongs. Which is the oldest of us three?
Facts sound like charges. The least important man
Is a legend in his neghbour's living-room,
Menacing and remarkable as the lightning
That ran from tree to tree about the house
So recently, like the shining of its ghosts,
I nod, but the names, perils, dates mean nothing.
And where thats true, the deepest bonds are lost.
How will the vine bear this year? I feel
My heart growing till my thoughts are hoarse
And the old branches pick at the heap of leavings.
There is so much I don't recall. They stand,
Timid, waving to watch me go, barely
Visible in the window's copper sheen.

FRANCIS WEBB(1925-1973)

Francis Charles Webb-was born Rose park,Adelaide, South Australia. Webb was an Australasian poet who published under the pen mane Francis Webb. Diagnosed suffering from schizophrenia in the 1950s he spent most of the adult life in and out of the mental hospitals.His output was prolific and the work often has been published in anthologies. His works are- *CollectedPoems*(1969), *DrumforBen Boyd*(1948)and *The Ghost of the Cock* (1964).

58. Harry

It's the day for writing that letter, if one is able,
And so the striped institutional shirt is wedged
Between this holy holy chair and table.
He has purloined paper, he has begged and cadged
The bent institutional pen,
The ink. And our droll old men
Are darting constantly where he weaves his sacrament.
Sacrifice? Propitiation? All are blent
In the moron's painstaking fingers—so painstaking.
His vestments our giddy yarns of the firmament,
Women, gods, electric trains, and our remaking
Of all known worlds—but not yet
Has our giddy alphabet
Perplexed his priest craft and spilled the
cruet of innocence
We have been plucked from the world of commonsense
Fondling between our hands some shining loot,
Wife, mother, beach fisticuffs, eloquence,
As the lank tree cherishes every distorted shoot
What queer shards we could steal
Shaped him, realer.

59. Wild Honey

Saboteur autumn has riddled the pampered folds
Of the sun; gum and willow whisper seditious things
Servile leaves now kick and toss in revolution,
Wave bunting, die in operatic reds and golds;
And we, the drones, fated for the hundred stings,
Grope among chilly combs of self-contemplation
While the sun, on sufferance, from his palanquin
Offers *creation one niggling lukewarm grin.*
But today is Sports Day, not a shadow of doubt:
Scampering at the actual frosty feet
Of winter, under shavings of the pensioned blue,
We are the Spring. True, rain is about:
You mark old diggings along the arterial street
Of the temples, the stuttering eyeball, the residue
Of days spent nursing some drugged comatose pain,
Summer, autumn, winter the single sheet of rain.
And the sun is carted off; and a sudden shower:
Lines of lightning patrol the temples of the skies;
Drum, thunder, silence sing as one this day;
Our faces return to the one face of the flower
Sodden and harried by diehard disconsolate flies.
All seasons are crammed into pockets of the grey.
Joy, pain, desire, a moment ago set free,
Sag in pavilions of the grey finality.
Under rain, in atrophy, dare I watch this girl
Combing her hair before the grey broken mirror,
The golden sweetness trickling? Her eyes show
Awareness of my grey stare beyond the swirl
Of golden fronds: it is her due. And terror,

Rainlike, is all involved in the golden glow,
Playing diminuendo its dwarfish role Between
self-conscious fingers of the naked soul.
Down with the mind a moment, and let Eden
Be fullness without the prompted unnatural hunger,
Without the doomed shapely ersatz thought: see faith
As all such essential gestures, unforbidden,
Persisting through Fall and landslip; and see, stranger,
The overcoated concierge of death As a toy for her gesture.
See her hands like bees Store golden combs
among certified hollow trees.
Have the gates of death scrape open. Shall we meet
(Beyond the platoons of rainfall) a loftier hill
Hung with such delicate husbandries? Shall ascent
Be a travelling homeward, past the blue frosty feet
Of winter, past childhood, past the grey snake, the will?
Are gestures stars in sacred dishevelment,
The tiny, the pitiable, meaningless and rare
As a girl beleaguered by rain, and her yellow hair?

BRUCE BEAVER (1928-2004)

Bruce Beaver was an Australia poet and novelist. He was born in Manly,New South Wales.He studied in Manley Public School and Sidney's Boys High School. He did lot of menial jobs-as a cow farmer, on radio station, as a wages clerk and labourer, fruit -picker,proof reader etc. He lived in New Zealand and Norfolk Island. His famous peoti al work *Charmed Lives*. His poetry was pungent, discursive, disturbing. He won Patrick White Award in 1982.

60. Exit

Behaviour is more human than we know.
All very well to quote the Book of Rules;
The catch is, if you stay, then I must go.
Some favour intermittence, some a flow;
The student keeps in touch with all the schools.
Behaviour is more human than we know.
Most fellow travellers vary fast with slow;
Adherence to a time-table soon cools.
The catch is, if you stay, then I must go.
The statistician hasn't got a show; .
Mere expertise in figures is for fools.
Behaviour is more human than we know.
The small rains fall, the little winds do blow.
A myriad tadpoles pullulate in pools.
The catch is, if you stay, then I must go.
Mergers may fail, though sense of oneness grow;
Psychology can leave behind its tools.
Behaviour is more human than we know.
The catch is, if you stay, then I must go.

61. Letters to Live Poets, I

God knows what was done to you.
I may never find out fully.
The truth reaches us slowly here,
is delayed in the mail continually
or censored in the tabloids. The war
now into its third year
remains undeclared.
The number of infants, among others, blistered
and skinned alive by napalm
has been exaggerated
by both sides we are told,
and the gas does not seriously harm
does not kill but is merely
unbearably nauseating.
Apparently none of this
is happening to us.
I meant to write to you more than a
ago. Then there was as much to hear,
as much to tell.
There was the black plastic monster
prefiguring hell
displayed on the roof
of the shark aquarium at the wharf.
At Surfers' Paradise were Meter Maids
glabrous in gold bikinis.
It was before your country's
president came among us like a formidable
virus. Even afterwards —
after I heard (unbelievingly)

you had been run down on a beach
by a machine
apparently while sunning yourself;
that things were terminal again —
even then I might have written.
But enough of that. I could tell by the tone
of your verses there were times
when you had ranged around you,
looking for a lift from the gift horse,
your kingdom for a Pegasus.
But to be trampled by the machine
beyond protest…
I don't have to praise you; at least
I can say I had ears for your voice
but none of that really matters now.
Crushed though. Crushed on the littered sands.
Given the *coup de grace* of an empty beer can,
out of sight of the "lordly and isolate satyrs".
Could it have happened anywhere else
than in your country, keyed to obsolescence?
I make these words perform for you
knowing though you are dead, that you "historically
belong to the enormous bliss of American death",
that your talkative poems remain
among the living things
of the sad, embattled beach-head.
Say that I am, as ever, the young-
old fictor of communications.
It's not that I wish to avoid
talking to myself or singing
the one-sided song.
It's simply that I've come to be
more conscious of the community

world-wide, of live, mortal poets.
Moving about the circumference
I pause each day
and speak to you and you.
I haven't many answers, few
enough; fewer questions left.
Even when I'm challenged "Who
goes there?" I give ambiguous
replies as though the self linking
heart and mind had become a gap.
You see, we have that much in common
already. It's only when I stop
thinking of you living I remember
nearby our home there's an aquarium
that people pay admission to,
watching sharks at feeding time:
the white, jagged rictus in the grey
sliding anonymity,
faint blur of red through green,
the continually spreading stain.
I have to live near this, if not quite with it.
I realize there's an equivalent
in every town and city in the world.
Writing to you keeps the local, intent
shark-watchers at bay
(who if they thought at all
would think me some kind of ghoul);
rings a bell for the gilded coin-slots
at the Gold Coast;
sends the president parliament's head on a platter;
writes Vietnam like a huge four-letter
word in blood and faeces on the walls
of government; reminds me when

the intricate machine stalls
there's a poet still living at this address.

PETER PORTER (1929-2010)

He was British-based Australian poet. He was born in Brisbane. He studied in Anglican Chruch Grammar School. He moved to England in 1951 and published more than 15 collection of poems. His works are-*The Last of England* (1970), *The Cost of Seriousness* (1978) and *Collected Poems*(1983) *Better thanGod*(2009).*Reston the Flight* (2010).

62. Your Attention, Please

The Polar DEW has just warned that
A nuclear rocket strike of
At least one thousand megatons
Has been launched by the enemy
Directly at our major cities.
This announcement will take
Two and a quarter minutes to make,
You therefore have a further
Eight and a quarter minutes
To comply with the shelter
Requirements published in the Civil
Defence Code – section Atomic Attack.
A specially shortened Mass
Will be broadcast at the end
Of this announcement-
Protestant and Jewish services
Will begin simultaneously-
Select your wavelength immediately
According to instructions
In the Defence Code. Do not
Take well-loved pets (including birds)
Into your shelter – they will consume
Fresh air. Leave the old and bed-
ridden, you can do nothing for them.
Remember to press the sealing
Switch when everyone is in
The shelter. Set the radiation
Aerial, turn on the geiger barometer.
Turn off your television now.

Turn off your radio immediately
The Services end. At the same time
Secure explosion plugs in the ears
Of each member of your family. Take
Down your plasma flasks. Give your children
The pills marked one and two
In the C.D. green container, then put
Them to bed. Do not break
The inside airlock seals until
The radiation All Clear shows
(Watch for the cuckoo in your
perspex panel), or your District
Touring Doctor rings your bell.
If before this, your air becomes
Exhausted or if any of your family
Is critically injured, administer
The capsules marked 'Valley Forge'
(Red pocket in No. 1 Survival Kit)
For painless death. (Catholics
Will have been instructed by their priests
What to do in this eventuality.)
This announcement is ending. Our President
Has already given orders for
Massive retaliation – it will be
Decisive. Some of us may die.
Remember, statistically
It is not likely to be you.
All flags are flying fully dressed
On Government buildings – the sun is shining.
Death is the least we have to fear.
We are all in the hands of God,
Whatever happens happens by His Will.
Now go quickly to your shelters.

63. Competition is Healthy Es wartet alles auf dich

Everything. Yes. Some men holy enough
To have seen the Buddha may try to keep
His commandments – to clothe the ragged in lightweight
Dacron, to feed the hungry with milk bread
Or curious corn, to press salve of the sacred
Laboratories of America into sores
Too big to form scabs. Yet the underprivileged
Rich pray for a Goldwater victory
Within an ant's tremor of God's instep.
Your heavenly Father knoweth that
Ye have need of all these things.
He gives bells that walk the fields
When the unsteady rice is shooting,
He gives Sebastian Bach to the citizens
Of Leipzig. Out of reach of the philharmonic
That old man is planting his garden.
He nestles each seedling in the soil,
Contrives a cotton grid to keep the sparrows off,
Sweats in conscience of his easy goal.
Unknown to him his son has scattered
Radish seed in the bed and the red clumsy
Tubers shall inherit the earth.
Take no thought saying 'What shall we eat?
What shall we drink? or Wherewithal shall
we be clothed?'
We shall eat the people we love,
We shall drink their fluids unslaked,

We shall dress in the flannel of their blood,
But we shall not go hungry or thirsty
Or cold. The old man writes with a post office nib
To his son. 'The Government has cut the quotas,
Here the bougainvillea is out,
The imported rose is sinking in the heat.'

BRUCE DAWE(1930-2020)

Donald Bruce Dawe AO was an Australian poet and academic. He was born in 1930 in Fitzroy, Victoria state. He had early education in North cote High School. Some critics consider him one of the most influential Australian poets of all time. Dawe received numerous poetry awards in Australia and was named an Officer of the Order of Australia. He taught literature in universities for over 30 years. His main works are- *Enter withoutso much as Knocking , Weapons Training,Sometimes Gladness and more.*

64. Life Cycle

When children are born in Victoria
they are wrapped in club-colours, laid in beribboned cots,
having already begun a lifetime's barracking.
Carn, they cry, Carn ... feebly at first
while parents playfully tussle with them
for possession of a rusk: Ah, he's a little Tiger!
(And they are ...)
Hoisted shoulder-high at their first League game
they are like innocent monsters who have been
years swimming
towards the daylight's roaring empyrean
Until, now, hearts sharpened with rapture,
they break surface and are forever lost,
their minds rippling out like streamers
In the pure flood of sound, they are scarfed with
light, a voice
like the voice of God booms from the stands
Oooh you bludger and the covenant is sealed.
Hot pies and potato-crisps they will eat,
they will forswear the Demons, cling to the Saints
and behold their team going up the ladder into Heaven,
And the tides of life will be the tides of the
home-team's fortunes
– the reckless proposal after the one-point win,
the wedding and honeymoon after the grand final ...
They will not grow old as those from the more
northern states grow old,
for them it will always be three-quarter time
with the scores level and the wind advantage in

the final term,
That passion persisting, like a race-memory,
through the welter of seasons,
enabling old-timers by boundary fences to
dream of resurgent lions
and centaur-figures from the past to replenish
continually the present,
So that mythology may be perpetually renewed
and Chicken Smallhorn return like the maize-god
in a thousand shapes, the dancers changing
But the dance forever the same – the elderly still
loyally crying Carn … Carn … (if feebly) unto
the very end,
having seen in the six-foot recruit from Eaglehawk
their hope of salvation

CHRIS-WALLACE-CRABBE
(1934-)

Christopher Keith Wallace Crabbe AM is an Australian poet and emeritus professor in the Australian Centre, University of Melbourne. His poetical works are- Mappings of the Plane, New Selected Poems, Author! Author!, Tales of Australian Literary Life.

65. Melbourne

Not on the ocean, on a muted bay
Where the broad rays drift slowly over mud
And flathead loll on sand, a city bloats
Between the plains of water and of loam.
If surf beats, it is faint and far away;
If slogans blow around, we stay at home.
And, like the bay, our blood flows easily.
Not warm, not cold (in all things moderate),
Following our familiar tides. Elsewhere
Victims are bleeding, sun is beating down
On patriot, guerrilla, refugee.
We see the newsreels when we dine in town.
Ideas are grown in other gardens while
This chocolate soil throws up its harvest of
Imported and deciduous platitudes.
None of them flowering boldly or for long:
And we, the gardeners, securely smile
Humming a bar or two of rusty song.
Old tunes are good enough if sing we must;
Old images, re-vamped ad nauseam.
Will sate the burgher's eye and keep him quiet
As the great wheels run on. And should he seek
Variety, there's wind, there's heat, there's frost
To feed his conversation all the week.
Highway be highway, the remorseless cars
Strangle the city, put it out of pain,
Its limbs still kicking feebly on the hills.
Nobody cares. The artists sail at dawn
For brisker ports, or rot in public bars.

Though much has died here, nothing has been born.

66. Nature, Language, the Sea: An Essay

But what of the artist: Has he either knowledge or correct belief?—

TheRepublic

With such worn currency of models as
Rivers and steps and roads, the mind
Does much of its diurnal labour;
Analogies its glory and its task,
Into the shambling mess we call
Creation it plunges, asking 'Why?'
For the world is wonder, is profusion,
A boundless brilliant orchard of
Sun-licked, thunder-shaken strangeness,
But nobody can claim it makes good sense
Or testifies to clarity:
O, the mistakes of a creator!
Nature, language, sea : our great examples
Of what must always be rebuked
By the modest radiance of art.
Where the thick ridges of a mountain range,
Ruffled with unbroken forest
And innocent of bridge or roadway,
Roll like a stiff surf out from under you
In one great Burkean rhythm
To shout, Sublime, Sublime, O Sublime,
And the gullies brim with a steely blue mist,

Is there, as your heart takes pause,
Anything heard but a hymn of chaos?
There are no sermons in the Great Divide;
The boundless overflows and Its tide is no river of symbols;
Yet symbols must rise glittering from some
Quick river or sullen current,
Dying as soon as their surface dries,
And sound roots must aspire from common soil
Earning a sudden right to bear
The fire-featured apples of the sun.
Nature, language, the sea; and opposite
These fluent fields of energy
Man feels that he is bound to chisel
The small hard statues of his poetry
Which bear, like a sheen on marble,
All the assurance of being right,
All the assurance that we come to know
Under the name of form, and know
In the strong humming of completeness
Wherein the formal is at last the good.
Both passionate and moral is
Music which has passed into a shape,
A river which has found its dimpling course
Through the golden fields of
Chronos, Sounding not of loss but clarity.

DAVID MALOUF (1934-)

David George Joseph Malouf AO is an Australasian poet, novelist, short story writer , playwright and liberal. He was the elected Fellow of the Royal Society of Literature in England in 2008. He lectured in both the University of Queensland and of Sydney. He also delivered te 1988 Boyer Lectures. His main works are- *BicycleandOtherPoems, Neighbors in a Thicket, Poems, Johnnno*. In 1974 he won the Grace Leven Prize for Poetry.

67. The Year of the Foxes

When I was ten my mother, having sold
her old fox-fur (a ginger red bone-jawed
Magda Lupescu
of a fox that on her arm played
dead, cunningly dangled
a lean and tufted paw)
decided there was money to be made
from foxes, and brought via
the columns of the Courier-Mail a whole
pack of them; they hung from penny hooks
in our paneled sitting-room, trailed from the backs
of chairs; and Brisbane ladies, rather
the worse for war, drove up in taxis wearing
a G.I. on their arm
and rang at our front door.
I slept across the hall, at night hearing
their thin cold cry. I dreamed the dangerous spark
of their eyes, brushes aflame
in our fur-hung, nomadic
tent in the suburbs, the dark fox-stink of them
cornered in their holes
and turning.
Among my mother's show pieces —
Noritake teacups, tall hock glasses
with stems like barley-sugar,
goldleaf demitasses —
the foxes, row upon row, thin-nosed, prick-eared,
dead.
The cry of hounds

was lost behind mirror glass,
where ladies with silken snoods and fingernails
of Chinese laquer red
fastened a limp paw;
went down in their high heels
to the warm soft bitumen, wearing at throat
and elbow the rare spoils
of '44; old foxes, rusty red like dried-up wounds,
and a G.I. escort.

RODNEY HALL(1935-)

Born in Slihuli, Warwickshire, England, he came to Australia as a child after the World War II and studied as a young man in the University of Queensland in 1971. He worked as an actor and also in Australian Broadcasting Commission., Brisbane. He edited The Australian a magazine between 1967 and 1978. He published 13 novels and some collection of poems. His main poetical works are- *The Climber*(1962), *Eyewitnesses*(1967), *TheLawofKarma*(1968), *SelectedPoems*(1975).

68. Heaven, in a Way

From my new world I'm waving.
See how far I've come?
Here it's perfectly alright
to turn however many somersaults you like
on all the roofs of town.
If anyone should care to live
in Gothic or in Romanesque cathedrals
thaf s alright too: you spread
your palliasse upon the altar or in the nave
and wake to find the morning sun
shattered to a flower of jewelled glass—
to find the ghost of a multicoloured
saint or two in bed beside you.
From my new world I'm waving.
See how far I've come?
It's no use being envious;
nothing but a life of heartbreak
can gain you entry to this place.
Here the fish are naturally disguised
with scales that read as Hebrew letters.
The smells of every intimate remembrance
play your mind on their hook and line,
until you do achieve a state of re-experience.
And the colours here lie warm against the eye:
film upon film of unforgotten pleasure.
I suppose it's heaven, in a way.
And I am waving down at you.
Ha ha! I hope you hate it where you are.
I see you—a grubby speck beneath me,

and if s all your own damned fault.
You don't know what you're missing.
Watch me exploit the magic
of my somersaulting powers. Up here
we're worshippers of education by experience;
with only another life of heartbreak still to go
before we accept ourselves, each as one of you.
From my new world I'm waving.
See how far I've come?

RANDOLPH STOW (1935-2010)

He, being known as Julian Randolph Stow, was a famous Australian poet. Born in Gerald ton, western Australia. He attended Guild ford Grammar School. He studied in the University of Western Australia and the University of Sydney. He taught in the university of Adelaide. His main poetical works are- *TotheIslands*(1958), *Tourmaline(*1963) and *The Merry-go-RoundintheSea*(1965). He won the Patrick White Award in 1979.

69. My Wish for my land

The Woman:
My wish for my land is that ladies be beautiful,
That horses be spirited and gentlemen courteous
And all mustaches faultless.
My wish for my husband is that he read Tennyson.
My wish for my daughter is that she be interesting
And capture a million acres.
My wish for my sons is that they be chivalrous,
sun-tanned and tall, and that they bestow on me'
Perhaps a dozen grandsons.
My wish for my house is that linen be Irish
And tableware sterling, and that the piano
Go never too long unplayed
My wish for myself is that I grow matronly,
Straying in dove-grey silk through the roses
Under the far far harking of the crows.
The Enemy
As well, maybe, that you cannot read our minds;
There are worse tools than swords and rifle-butts.
My enemy: my passion. At dead of night,
Licking my wounds, I begin to think I love you.
Certainly none were ever so bound in love
As we are bound in hate: O my ideal.
One sight of you, and life grows meaningful.
One blow: new strength to every slave who watches;
One word: revived fidelity, fresh lust.
Time-weakness – absence – death can have no bearing.
You whom I serve, your perfect gentle knight,
Can you divine that longed-for consummation?

Lover: I mean to take you like a sponge,
And wring your blood out on Hiroshima.

LES MURRAY (1938-2019)

Leslie Allan Murray AO was an Australian poet, anthologist and critic. His career spanned over 40 years and he published nearly 30 volumes of poetry as well as two prose verse novels and collections of his prose writings. He studied in Taree High School and later in the University of Sydney . His main works are- *FreddyNeptune*, (1998), *Collected Poems* (1991), *TheIlexTree*(1965), *Subhuman Redneck*(1996), and *Continuous Creation* (1996)

70. The Wilderness

For Peter Barden
Penury in Sydney had grown stale
And, at twenty-two, my childhood was in danger
So I preceded you, in all but spirit,
To the far-back country
Where the tar roads end.
In the silent lands
Time broadens into space.
Approaching Port Augusta, going on,
Iron-brown and limitless, the plains
Were before me all day. Burnt mountains fell behind
In the glittering sky.
At dawn, the sun would roll up from his lair
In the kiln-dry lake country, fire his heat straight through
The blind grey scrub, awaken me beside wheeltracks
And someone's car, and I would travel on.
At noon, far out in a mirage, I would brew
Tea with strangers, yarn about jobs in the North
And, chewing quietly, watch may be an upstart
Dust-devil forming miles off, going high
To totter, darken
And, quite suddenly, vanish
Leaving a formless, thinning stain in the heavens.
Where the spirits of sea-cliffs Hovered on the plain
I would remember routines we had invented
For putting spine into shapeless days: the time
We passed at a crouching trot down Wynyard Concourse
Tell each other in loud mock-Arunta and gestures
What game we were tracking down what

haunted gorge...
Frivolous games
But they sustained me like water,
They, and the is-ful ah!-nesses of things.

71. The Two Sisters

Related by Manoowa

On the Island of the Spirits of the Dead,
one of two sisters talks.
'We must make a canoe
and follow the way the sun walks'.
They've filled the canoe with sacred
rannga things,
and paddled away into the night
singing ritual songs.
'Sister, look back!' the first sister calls.
Do you see the morning star?'
Her sister looks out along their wake. '
Nothing. Nothing₇s there.'
The little sister has fallen asleep.
Again her sister calls,
'Sister, look back for the morning star.'
'Nothing, Nothing at all.'
A spear of light is thrown across
the sea and lies far
ahead upon the sister's course.
'Sister, the morning star.'
The sun comes up and walks the sky.
A fish with whiskers swims
ahead, and leaps out of the sea,
while the sisters sing.
Day and night, and day and night,
the sisters are gone

with the morning star and the leaping fish
and the sky-walking sun.
The sisters, hoar with dried salt spray,
Thesemen of the sea,
make landfall whereparrots scream
from paperbark trees.
The sisters beach the bark canoe,
unload the rannga things.
They thrust one in the earth. From there
the first goanna comes.
They've gone inland. Their digging sticks
make sacred springs.
They leave behind them rannga forms
for all living things.
Out gathering food, the sisters have hung
their dilly-bags in a tree.
While they're away, men come and steal
their sacred ceremonies.
The sisters hear men singing
and song-sticks' 'tjong-tjong'.
'Cover your ears. We cannot hear
the sacred song.'
'O, all our sacred ceremonies
belong now to the men.
We must gather food, and bear
and rear children.'

72. The Wild Colonial Boy

ANONYMOUS

'Tis of a wild Colonial Boy, Jack Doolan was his name,
Of poor but honest parents he was born in Castlemaine.
He was his father's only hope, his mother's pride and joy,
And dearly did his parents love the wild Colonial Boy.
Chorus
Come, all my hearties, we'll roam the mountains high,
Together we will plunder, together we will die.
We'll wander over valleys, and gallop over plains,
And we'll scorn to live in slavery, bound down
with iron chains.
He was scarcely sixteen years of age when he left
his father's home,
And through Australia's sunny clime a bushranger
did roam.
He robbed those wealthy squatters, their stock he
did destroy,
And a terror to Australia was the wild Colonial Boy.
In sixty-one this daring youth commenced his wild
career,
With a heart that knew no danger, no foeman did he fear.
He stuck up the Beechworth mail-coach, and robbed
Judge MacEvoy,
Who trembled, and gave up his gold to the wild Colonial Boy.
He bade the judge "Good morning", and told him to
beware,
That he'd never rob a hearty chap that acted on the

square,
And never to rob a mother of her son and only joy,
Or else you might turn outlaw, like the wild Colonial Boy.
One day as he was riding the mountain-side along,
A-listening to the little birds, their pleasant laughing song,
Three mounted troopers rode along
-Kelly, Davis, and FitzRoy -
They thought that they would capture him, the wild
Colonial Boy.
"Surrender now, Jack Doolan, you see there's three to one.
Surrender now, Jack Doolan, you're a daring
highwayman."
He drew a pistol from his belt, and shook the little toy,
"I'll fight, but not surrender," said the wild Colonial Boy.
He fired at Trooper Kelly and brought him to the ground,
And in return from Davis received a mortal wound.
All shattered through the jaws he lay still firing at FitzRoy,
And that's the way they captured him - the wild Colonial Boy.

73. Dunn, Gilbert and Ben Hall

Come all ye wild colonials And listen to my tale;
A story of bushrangers' deeds I will to you unveil.
'Tis of those gallant heroes, Game fighters one and all;
And we'll sit and sing, Long Live the King,
Dunn,Gilbert, and Ben Hall.
Ben Hall he was a squatter bloke Who owned a thousand
head;
A peaceful man he was until Arrested by Sir Fred.
His home burned down, his wife cleared out,
His cattle perished all;
"They'll not take me a second time,'
Says valiant Ben Hall.
John Gilbert was a flash cove, And John O'Meally too;
With Ben and Bourke and Johnny Vane
They all were comrades true.
They rode into Canowindra And gave a public ball.
'Roll up, roll up, and have a spree,'
Says Gilbert and Ben Hall.
They took possession of the town, Including the public-
houses,
And treated all the cockatoos And shouted for their
spouses.
They danced with all the pretty girls And held a carnival.
'We don't hurt them who don't hurt us,'
Says Gilbert and Ben Hall.
They made a raid on Bathurst, The pace was getting hot;
But Johnny Vane surrendered After Micky Burke was
shot,
O'Meally at Goimbla Did like a hero fall;

'The game is getting lively,'
Says John Gilbert and Ben Hall.
Then Gilbert took a holiday, Ben Hall got new recruits;
The Old Man and Dunleavy Shared in the plunder's fruits.
Dunleavy he surrendered And they jagged the Old Man
tall -
So Johnny Gilbert came again
To help his mate Ben Hall.
John Dunn he was a jockey bloke, A-riding all the
winners,
Until he joined Hall's gang to rob The publicans and
sinners;
And many a time the Royal Mail Bailed up at John Dunn's
call.
A thousand pounds is on their heads -
Dunn, Gilbert, and Ben Hall.
'Next week we'll visit Goulburn And clean the banks out
there;
So if you see the troopers, Just tell them to beware;
Some day to Sydney city We mean to pay a call,
And we'll take the whole damn country,'
Says Dunn, Gilbert, and Ben Hall.

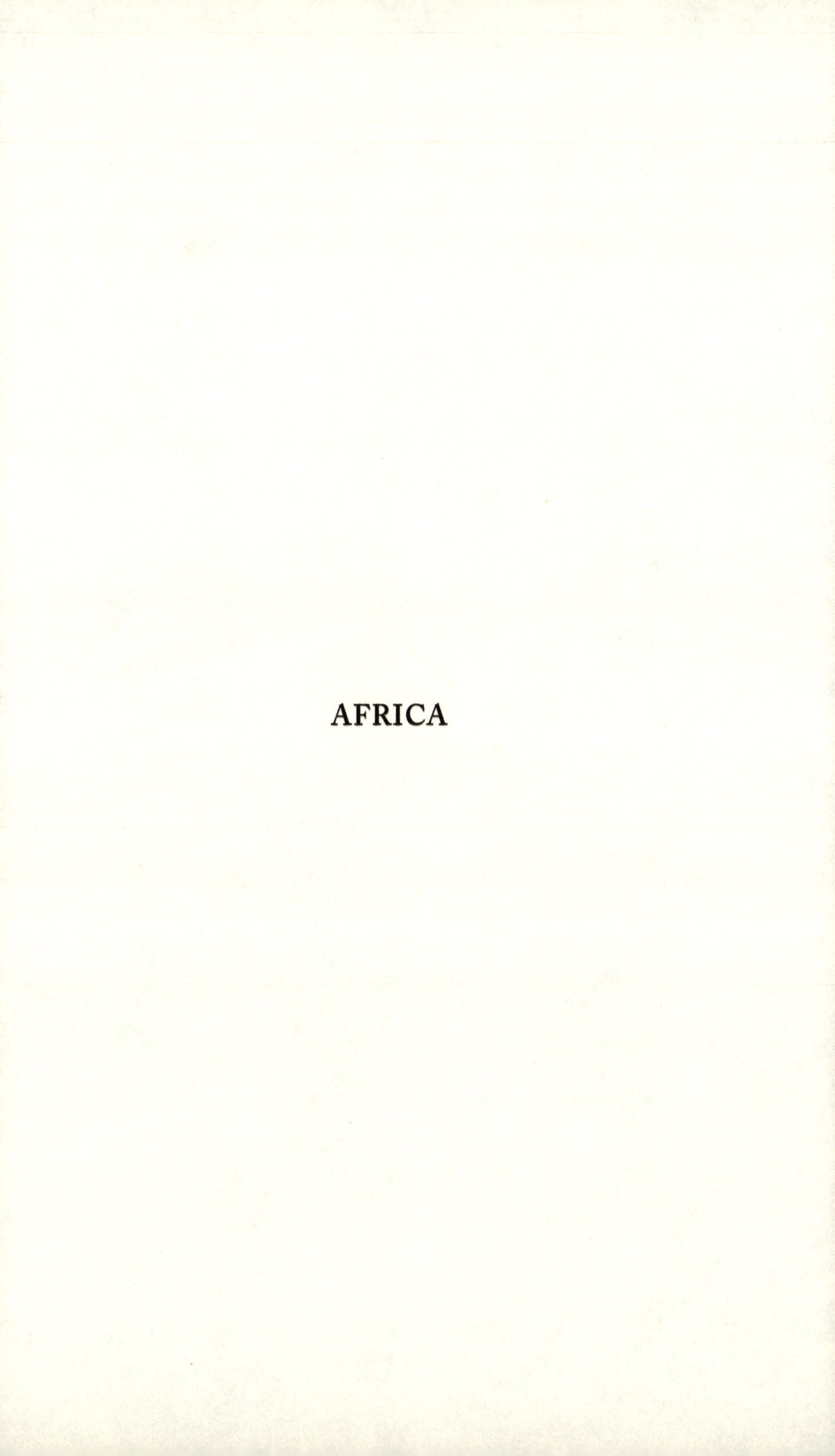

AFRICA

FLAVIEN RANAIVO (1914-1999)

Flavien Ranaivo is a Madagascar lyrical poet and a prolific writer. He was born in 1914 in Arivonimamo, in Madagascar. He began his education at the age of 8. His father died two years of his birth. His schooling was Malagasy. His main work is Bending the Bow: An Anthology of African Love Poetry and it was edited by F.M. Chipusula.

74. Song of a Young girl

Of
tlie young man who lives down there
beside the threshing floor for rice;
like two banana-roots
on either side the village ditch,
we gaze on each other,
we are lovers,
but he won't marry me.
Jealous
his mistress I saw two days since at the wash house
coming down the path against the wind.
She was proud;
was it because she wore a lamba thick
and studded with coral
or because they are newly bedded?
However it isn't the storm
that will flatten the delicate reed,
nor the great sudden shower
at the passage of a cloud
that will startle out of his wits
the blue bull.
I am amazed;
the big sterile rock
survived the rain of the flood,
and it's the fire that crackles
the bad grains of maize.
Such this famous smoker
who took tobacco
when there was no more hemp to burn.

A foot of hemp?
- Sprung in Andringitra,
spent in Ankaratra,
no more than cinders to us.
False flattery
stimulates love a little
but the blade has two edges;
why change what is natural?
- If I have made you sad
look at yourself in the water of repentance,
you will decipher there a word I have left.
Good-bye, whirling puzzle,
I give you my blessing:
wrestle with the crocodile,
here are your victuals and three water-lily flowers
for the way is long.

BERNARD DADIE (1916-2019)

Bernard Binlin Dadie was an Ivorian novelist , playwright, poet ,and administrator. He was born in Assassin-Mafia, Cote d'ivorie. Among many other senior positions starting 1957. He held the post of Minister for Culture in the government of Cote d'ivorie from 1977 to 1986. His main poetical works are-*The BlackCloth*, *Climbie*, and *An African in Paris*.

75. I Thank You God

I thank you God for creating me Black,
For making of me
Porter of all sorrows,
Setting on my head
The World.
I wear the Centaur's hide
And I have carried the World since the first morning.
White is a colour for special occasions
Black is the colour for every day
And I have carried the World since the first evening.
I am glad
Of the shape of my head
Made to carry the World,
Content
With the shape of my nose
That must snuff every wind of the World
Pleased
With the shape of my legs
Ready to run all the heats of the World.
I thank you God for creating me black
For making of me
Porter of all sorrows.
Thirty-six swords have pierced my heart.
Thirty-six fires have burnt my body.
And my blood on all calvaries has reddened the snow,
And my blood at every dawn has reddened all nature.
Still I am
Glad to carry the World,
Glad of my short arms

of my long arms
of the thickness of my lips.
I thank you God for creating me black.
White is the colour for special occasions
Black the colour for every day
And I have carried the World since the dawn of time.
And My laugh over the World, through the night,
creates the Day.
I thank you God for creating me black.

JEAN JOSEPH REBEARIVELO
(1901-1937)

He was born Jean- Joseph Rabearivelo-Casmir Rabearivelo was a
Malagasy poet who is widely considered to be the first modern poet and
te greatest literary artist of Madagascar. His main works are-
AlmostDreams(1960), *Translationsfrom the Malagasy* and
CompeteLaterPoetry of Jean JosephRabearivelo.

76. Three Birds

The bird of iron the bird of steel
That rent the morning clouds
And wanted to snatch the stars
Is hiding shamefully
Beyond day
In an unreal cave.
The bird of flesh the bird of feathers
That thrust a tunnel through he wind
In quest of the moon whom he saw in his dreams
Hanging in the branches
Plunges like the evening
Into a thicket of leaves
But he who is without body
Bewitches the guardian of skulls
With his stammering song
He opens his sounding wings
Hurries to pacify space
And only returns immortal.

RICHARD NTIRU (1946-)

Richard Ntiru was a famous African poet. He was born in Kisoro in Kigezidistrict in south western Uganda. 1946. His only Collection of poems - is Tensions (1971). His poetry is rich in imagery reminiscent of the poetry of Christopher Okigbo and Paul Ndu. He dealt with the issues of Contemporary East Africa, exploring the divisions in the human society and criticizes the attitude towards the unfortunate.

77. The Shapes of Fear

Like an arrested breath
when breathing makes silence imperfect
and the ear cannot differentiate
between the conspiratorial whispers and the winds
singing.
... a twig in the courtyard snaps
and report of a gun is understood.
Like the suspended step
When a mouldy piece of wood lies across the path
And the wary eye cannot separate
The snake supple slipperiness from the clumsy presence
The lone traveler sees the marriage on the road
And thinks again of Noah and the Flood.
Like the drawn vacuum moment
When the inmate half expectantly says Karibu
And the eye relieves the ear
To welcome the caller who does not enter
The late homecomer sees
Baringa at night
And suspects assassins all along the path.
Like the timid child's time
Between the deed and the summons
Between the incidental slip of the tongue
And the roaring presence of the harsh mother
A loose pane falls from its frame
And the tenant has to look for a new house
Like this and so much more
In this nauseating odour of human mockery..

DENNIS BRUTUS (1924—2009)

Dennis Brutus was born in Salisbury, southern Rhodesia. He got his education in the University of Fort Hare (B.A.1946) and the University of the Wit water sand. He was a famous the south African poet, activist, and educationist, journalist and poet best known for his campaign to have South Africa banned from the Olympics Games due to its racial policy of the Apartheid. The only work about is Dennis Brutus Tapes: Essays at Autobiography, edited by Bernth Lindfors.

78. A Common Hate Enriched Our Love and Us

Escape to parasitic ease disgusts;
discreet expensive hushes stifled us
the plangent wines became acidulous
Rich foods knotted to revolting clots
of guilt and anger in our queasy guts
remembering the hungry comfortless.
In draughty angles of the concrete stairs
or seared by salt winds under brittle stars
we found a poignant end to tenderness,
and, sharper than our strain, the passion
against our land's disfigurement and tension;
hate gouged out deeper levels for our passion -
a common hate enriched our love for us.

79. You Laughed and Laughed and Laughed

In your ears my song
is motor car misfiring
stopping with a choking cough;
and you laughed and laughed and laughed.
In your eyes my ante-
natal walk was inhuman, passing
your 'omnivorous understanding'
and you laughed and laughed and laughed
You laughed at my song,
you laughed at my walk.
Then I danced my magic dance
to the rhythm of talking drums pleading, but you shut
your eyes
and laughed and laughed and laughed
And then I opened my mystic
inside wide like the sky,
instead you entered your
car and laughed and laughed and laughed
You laughed at my dance,
you laughed at my inside.
You laughed and laughed and laughed.
But your laughter was ice-block
laughter and it froze your inside froze
your voice froze your ears
froze your eyes and froze your tongue.
And now it's my turn to laugh;
but my laughter is not

ice-block laughter. For I
know not cars, know not ice-blocks.
My laughter is the fire
of the eye of the sky, the fire
of the earth, the fire of the air,
the fie of the seas and the
rivers fishes animals trees
and it thawed your inside,
thawed your voice, thawed your
ears, thawed your eyes and
thawed your tongue.
So a meek wonder held
your shadow and you whispered;
'Why so?'
And I answered:
Because my fathers and I
'are owned by the living
warmth of the earth
through our naked feet.'

CHRISTOPHER OKIGBO
(1932-1967)

Christopher Ifekandu Okigbo was a Nigerian poet teacher and librarian was born in Ojoto Anambra State and died in Nsukka fighting for the independence of Biafra. He is today widely acknowledged as an outstanding post colonial English language African poet. And one of the major modern 20[th]century writers. His main works are- *Labyrinths, withthe PathofThunder*(1971), *PathofThunder*(1968) and *Collected Poems*(1986).

80. Heavensgate

The Passage
BEFORE YOU, my mother Idoto,
Naked I stand;
Before your weary presence,
A prodigal
Leaning on an oilbean,
Lost in your legend
Under your power wait I
On barefoot,
Watchman for the watchword
At Heavensgate;
Out of the depth my cry:
Give ear and hearken…
DARK WATERS of the beginning.
Ray, violet, and short, piercing the gloom,
Foreshadow the fire that is dreamed of.
Rainbow on far side, arched like boa bent to kill,
Foreshadow the fire that is dreamed of.
Me to the orangery
Solitude invites,
A wagtail, to tell
The tangled-wood-tale;
A sunbird, to mourn
A mother on spray.
Rain and sun in single combat;
On one leg standing,
In silence at the passage
The young bird at the passage
SILENCE FACES at crossroads:

Festivity in black...
Faces of black like black
Column of ants,
Behind the bell tower,
Into the hot garden
Where all roads meet:
Festivity in black...
O Anan at the knob of the panel oblong,
Hear us at crossroads at the great hinges
Where the players of loft organ
Rehearse old lovely fragment, alone-
Strains of pressed orange leaves on pages
Bleach of the light of years held in leather:
For we are listening in cornfields
Among the windplayers,
Listening to the wind leaning over
Its loveliest fragment....
Newcomer
Time for worship—
softly sing the bells of exile, the angelus,
softly sings my guardian angel.
Mask over my face—
my own mask, not ancestral—I sing:
remembrance of cavalry, and of age
of innocence, which is of... Time for worship:
ANNA OF THE PANEL OBLONGS,
PROTECT ME
FROM THEM FUCKING ANGELS:
PROTECT ME
MY SANDHOUSE AND BONES.
FOR GEORGETTE
IN THE CHILL breath of the day's
waking comes the newcomer,

when the draper of May
has sold out fine green garments,
and the hillsides have made up their faces,
and the gardens, on their faces a painted smile:
such synthetic welcome at the cock's third siren;
when from behind the bulrushes
waking, in the teeth of the chill May morn,
come the newcomer.
I am standing above the noontide,
above the bridgehead;
listening to the laughter of waters
that do not know why;
listening to incense—
1
am standing above the noontide
with my head above it;
under my feet float the waters
Tide blows them under..

GABRIEL OKARA (1921-2019)

He was a great Nigerian poet and novelist who was born in Bumoundi , Yenagoa, Bayelsa state, Nigeria. He was educated first in Government College Umuahia and later in the North-western University. He was a great poet essayist, writer and playwright. His notable work is The *Voice (1964), The Fisherman'sInvocation*(1978), *Collected Poems* (2016), and *TheDreamer-HisVision:Poems*(2004).

81. Once Upon a Time

Once upon a time, son,
they used to laugh with their hearts
and laugh with their eyes:
but now they only laugh with their teeth,
while their ice-block-cold eyes
search behind my shadow.
There was a time indeed
they used to shake hands with their hearts:
but that's gone, son.
Now they shake hands without hearts
while their left hands search
my empty pockets.
'Feel at home!' 'Come again':
they say, and when I come
again and feel
at home, once, twice,
there will be no thrice-
for then I find doors shut on me.
So I have learned many things, son.
I have learned to wear many faces
like dresses – homeface,
officeface, streetface, hostface,
cocktailface, with all their conforming smiles
like a fixed portrait smile.
And I have learned too
to laugh with only my teeth
and shake hands without my heart.
I have also learned to say,' Goodbye',
when I mean 'Good-riddance':

to say 'Glad to meet you',
without being glad; and to say 'It's been
nice talking to you', after being bored.
But believe me, son.
I want to be what I used to be
when I was like you. I want
to unlearn all these muting things.
Most of all, I want to relearn
how to laugh, for my laugh in the mirror
shows only my teeth like a snake's bare fangs!
So show me, son,
how to laugh; show me how
I used to laugh and smile
once upon a time when I was like you.

82. Were I to Choose

"When Adam broke the stone
and red streams raged down to
gather in the womb,
an angel calmed the storm",
"And I, the breath mewed
in Cain, unblinking gaze
at the world without
from the brink of an age".
That draws from the groping lips
A breast muted cry
To thread the years
(O were I to choose)
And now the close of one
And thirty turns, the world
Of bones is Babel, and the different tongues within
Are flames the head
Continually burning.
And O of this dark halo
Were the tired head free.
And when the harmattan
Of days has parched the throat
And skin, and sucked the fever
Of the head away.
Then the massive dark
descends, and flesh and bone
are razed. And (O were I
to choose) I'd cheat the worms
and silence seek in stone.

83. The Mystic Drum

The mystic drum in my inside
and fishes danced in the rivers
and men and women danced on land
to the rhythm of my drum
But standing behind a tree
with leaves around her waist
she only smiled with a shake of her head.
Still my drum continued to beat,
rippling the air with quickened
tempo compelling the quick
and the dead to dance and sing
with their shadows –
But standing behind a tree
with leaves around her waist
she only smiled with a shake of her head.
Then the drum beat with the
rhythmof the things of the ground
and invoked the eye of the sky
the sun and the moon and the river gods –
and the trees bean to dance,
the fishes turned menand men
turned fishesand things stopped to grow –
But standing behind a tree
with leaves around her waist
she only smiled with a shake of her head.
And then the mystic drum
in my inside stopped to beat –
and men became men,
fishes became fishes

and trees, the sun and the moon
found their places, and the dead
went to the ground and things began to grow.
And behind the tree she stoodwith roots
sprouting from herfeet and leaves growing
on her headand smoke issuing from her
noseand her lips parted in her smileturned
cavity belching darkness.Then, then I
packed my mystic drumand turned away;
never to beat so loud any more.

DAVID RUBADIRI (1930-2018)

David Rubadiri was also known as James David Rubadri lukin Hendricks was a Malawian poet , academic and diplomat educated Kings College, Cambridge and later in the University of Bristol, Maker ere University. He was also playwright and novelist. He is ranked as one of the major poets to emerge after the independence. His main works are- *Growing upwithPoetry*(1989) and *AnAfrican Thunderstorm& Other Poems*(2004).

84. A Negro Labourer in Liverpool

I have passed him
Slouching on dark backstreet pavements
Head bowed—
Taut, haggard and worn.
A dark shadow amidst dark shadows.
I have lifted my face to his,
Our eyes met
But on his dark negro face
No sunny smile,
No hope or longing for a hope promised;
Only the quick cowed dart of eyes
Piercing through impassive crowds
Searching longingly for a face
Feeling painfully for a heart
That might flicker understanding.
This is him—
The negro labourer in Liverpool
That from his motherland, A heart heavy
With the load of a century's oppression,
Gloriously sought for an identity
Grappled to clutch the fire of manhood
In the land of the free. But here are only the free
dead—
For they too are groping for a light.
Will that sun
That greeted him from his mother's womb
Ever shine again? Not here—
Here his hope is the shovel,
And his fulfilment resignation.

ARTHUR NORTJE (1942-2010)

Arthur Nortje was born in Oudtshoorn, South Africa. He was educated at Jesus College, Oxford. And University College of Western Cope. He studied under Dennis Brutus, the famous poet. Then he emigrated to Canada in 1967 and taught in Toronto. *Dead Roots* (1973) is only work. *Anatomy of Dark: The CollectedPoemsof Arthur Nortje* was edited by Dirk Klopper.

85. Letter from Pretoria Central Prison

The bell wakes me at 6 in the pale spring dawn
with the familiar rumble of the guts negotiating
murky corridors that smell of bodies. My eyes
find salutary the insurgent light of distances.
Waterdrops rain crystal cold, my wet
face in ascent from an iron basin
greets its rifled shadow in the doorway.
They walk us to the workshop. I am eminent,
the blacksmith of the block: these active hours
fly like sparks in the furnace, I hammer metals
with zest letting the sweating muscles
forge a forgetfulness of worlds more magnetic.
The heart, being at rest, life peaceable,
your words filter softly through my fibres.
Taken care of, in no way am I unhappy,
being changed to neutral. You must decide
today, tomorrow, bear responsibility,
take gaps in pavement crowds, refine ideas.
Our food we get on time. Most evenings
I read books, Jane Austen
for elegance, agreeableness (Persuasion).
Trees are green beyond the wall, leaves through the
mesh
are cool in sunshine
among the monastic white flowers of spring that floats
prematurely across the exercise yard, a square
of the cleanest stone I have ever walked on.

Sentinels smoke in their boxes, the wisps
curling lovely through the barbed wire.
Also music and cinema, yesterday double feature.
At 4 PM if s back to the cell, don't laugh
to hear how accustomed one becomes. You spoke
of hospital treatment—I see smart nurses
bringing you grapefruit and tea—good
luck to the troublesome kidney.

TSEGAYE GABRE -MEDKIN
(1936-2006)

Tsegaye gabre -medkin was an Ethiopian poet and novelist. He was born in 1936 in Bodaa village, near Ambo, Ethiopias some 120 km from the capital city of Addis Ababa. He is part Amhara and part Oramo tribes. His novels and poetry evoke retrospective narratives and fanciful epics. His books were commercially successful. His work is solely based in Amharic and English languages. His works are- *Tewdros, Petrosat the Hour,* and *TheOdaOakOracle.*He died in New York, USA.

86. Home- Coming Son

Look where you walk unholy stranger
This is the land of the eighth harmony
In the rainbow: Black. It is the dark side of the moon
Brought to light
This is the canvas of God's master stroke.
Out, of your foreign outfit unholy stranger
Feel part of the great work of art Walk in peace,
walk alone, walk tall, Walk free, walk naked
Let the feelers of your motherland
Caress your bare feet
Let Her breath kiss your naked body.
But watch, watch where you walk forgotten stranger
This is the very depth of your roots: Black
Where the tom-toms of your fathers vibrated
In the fearful silence of the valleys
Shook, in the colossus bodies of the mountains
Hummed, in the deep chest of the jungles.
Walk proud.
Watch, listen to the calls of the ancestral spirits
prodigal son
To the call of the long awaited soil
They welcome you home, home. In the song of birds
You hear your suspended family name
The winds whisper the golden names of your tribal
warriors
The fresh breeze blown onto your nostrils
Floats their bones turned to dust. Walk tall.
The spirits welcome
Their lost-son returned.

Watch, and out of your foreign outfit brother
Feel part of the work of art Walk in laughter,
walk in rhythm, walk tall Walk free, walk naked.
Let the roots of your motherland caress your body
Let the naked skin absorb the home-sun and shine
ebony.

NOEMIA DE SOUSA (1926-2002)

Noemia de Sousa is a famous African poetess. Carolina Noémia Abranches de Sousa Soares, known as Noémia de Sousa, was a poet from Mozambique who wrote in the Portuguese language. She was also known as Vera Micaia. She was of mixed Portuguese and Bantu descent. *Sangue Negro*, Maputo: Associação dos Escritores Moçambicanos, 2001. Her main work is - Margaret Busby (ed.), *Daughters of Africa* (1992).

87. If You Want to Know Me

If you want to know me
examine with careful eyes
this bit of black wood
which some unknown Makeonde brother
cut and carved
with his inspired hands
in the distant lands of the North.
This is what I am
empty sockets despairing of possessing life
a mouth torn open in an anguished wound
huge hands outspread
and raised in imprecation and in threat
a body tattooed with wounds seen and unseen
from the harsh whip strokes of slavery
tortured and magnificent
proud and mysterious
Africa from head to foot
This is what I am.
If you want to understand me
come, bend over this soul of Africa
in the black dockworker's groans
the Chope's frenzied dances
the Changanas' rebellion
in the strange sadness which flows
from an African song, through the night
And ask no more to know me
for I'm nothing but a shell of flesh where
Africa's revolt congealed
its cry pregnant with hope.

TEHICAYA U.TAM'SI (1931-1988)

Tchicaya U Tam'si was born in Mpil, Brazzaville, Congo. He moved to Paris in 1946 with his father and spent his childhood there. He was a Congolese author; his pen name means "small paper that speaks for its country" in Kikongo. His main works are - *The Belly, Selected Poems*(1970) and *The MadmanandtheMedusa*(1986).

88. Agony

There is no better key to dreams
than my name sang a bird
in a lake of blood
the sea danced alongside
dressed in blue-jeans
blowing the squalling gulls to bits
a black boatman
who claimed to know the stars
said he could cure with the mud of his sad eyes
the lepers of their leprosy
if a tonic love would unloose his arms
my name is key to dreams I am not leprous
take me across this river before you speak my
name and your arms will be unloosed
I hold the singing oar
where is this river I must cross
is it that lake of blood
follow me close your eyes think of the moon
contemplate my river and let us cross
the man and the bird sang
steered three days three nights to cross
the dirty bed of a river
listen
the wave rocks the boatman he sleeps he dreams
a charnel house offers a feast where his bowels are
eaten first then his arms then his memory
where the putrid bodies eat each other by the glimmer
of fire-flies which each carries at his temples
striving to resemble the christian god

there where they drink the slow song of the nightingale
one innocent pities his legs
scrapes from the bowl of ebony-wood
the last scrap of his memory
rope dancer on the thread of low-water mark
He knows the love which opposes his
pain the nightmares of the boatman in his
troubled sleep the wings of the birds who float their
anthem and who row too happily over the singing
water
on the far bank the plain comes to drink with its
troops of wild grasses bellowing their thirst in
a tropical rhythm while the peevish sun stabs at them
the sun pricks the side of the fisherman
his swords all newly forged
all newly tempered with blood
and this blood oozes from the earth and trickles
from the sky on a night of yellow rain
the boatman tells his name to be quail
no my name is key to dreams I am not leprous
quail is not my name do not die awaiting me
I am your soul farewell
my dark body farewell
your arms will unloose themselves
I am not leprous
do not die awaiting me
arms opened in a cross

CHINUA ACHEBE (1930-2013)

Chinua Achebewas a Nigerian novelist , poet and critic who is regarded as a central figure of modern African literature. His first novel *Things Fall Apart* occupies pivotal place in African literature and remains the most widely read, translated and studied African novel. His main poetical works are -Beware Soul brother and Other Poems(1972).Christmas in Biafraand Other Poems (1973).

89. Refugee Mother and Child

No Madonna and Child could touch
that picture of a mother's tenderness
for a son she soon would have to forget.
The air was heavy with odours
of diarrhoea of unwashed children
with washed-out ribs and dried-up
bottoms struggling in laboured
steps behind blown empty bellies. Most
mothers there had long ceased
to care but not this one; she held
a ghost smile between her teeth
and in her eyes the ghost of a mother's
pride as she combed the rust-coloured
hair left on his skull and then -
singing in her eyes - began carefully
to part it... In another life this
would have been a little daily
act of no consequence before his
breakfast and school; now she
did it like putting flowers
on a tiny grave.

LENRIE PETERS (1932-2009)

Lenrie Peters was born in 1932 in Bathurst, Gambia. He was a surgeon, novelist, poet, and educationist. He studied at Trinity College, Cambridge, England. His main collections of poetry are- *Poems*(1964), *Satellites*(1967), *Katchika*i(1967) and *Selected Poetry*(1981).

90. On a Wet September Morning

On a wet September morning
When vultures hate themselves
On the beach, against the flooded moorage
Along the rock shelves
Where sea-gulls lay their eggs.
Half under the cracking waves
With sea-weed under my nails
Where the coastline bends.
The sea was not the land's end.
The world under the sea
The sea under the earth
The sky under the sea
Were elemental changes of a world.
As the true life is death
Which is the idea inside us
So distinction ends.
The plagued centuries
In a weeping jelly-fish.
The pebble that will be a crown
The moon reflected in a starfish.
My amputated feet
Buried in soft sand
Within the blue shadows
Were already prehistoric.
I tried to leap
Out of shark's way
Far from the cutting teeth
Thundering like the wave
Aimed at my vitals, not my feet

But they had planted roots
Among the symbiosing weeds
Which issued from my feet
Under the caressing current
Where disproportionate time
Lulled in deep sleep.
I could not move;
I say I could not move
My vegetable feet,
But still the tumbling jaws.
Only a silent yell
Rang through time's corridors
To the farthest end
Where the amoeba becomes
The fire, water and air.
Where the primeval fruit still hangs.
So to the other end
Where plants are but continents
Deep in the future
That is darker and older
Than the past.
The echo burst inside me
Like a great harmonic chord—
Violins of love and happy voices
The pagan trumpet blast
Swamping the lamentation of the hom
Then the heraldic drums
In slow crescendo rising
crashed through my senses
Into a new present
Which is the future.
It was the music
Floating on salt air

Mixture of ozone and fish, urea
Boundless in all her forms
Like children's toys
Which lifted me
Higher than myself
From the palsied hand of destruction.
In the new vibrations
Came new awareness
And care born of feeling
Fear, and the pestilence of thought
Was cradled in a wet pulsating stone.
How then the smell of fish
The salted lips
Were like violets in a desert waste
The rancid taste
Her priceless treasury of gems,
Hot burning sands
Like the edentulous
Sprouting palms.
The sea was the desert
The wet was the dry
Here was there.
All indistinguishable
Like the smell of
Old men's trousers
From the Sunday joint
Truth lay on the sea bed
Black suffering on the land.
The sun raised gently her head
As I lay buried on the sand.

BIRAGO DIOP (1906-1989)

Birago Diop was born in Ouekam in 1906, outside Dakar , Senegal. He was an African Francophone poet and story teller.. He was encouraged by his family in young age to pursue his studies. He is known for his small but beautifully composed output of lyrical poetry with his compatriot Leopold Sedar Senghor. His only collection of poems is *Lures and Glimmers* (1960).

91. Breath

Listen more to things
Than to words that are said.
The water's voice sings
And the flame cries
And the wind that brings
The woods to sighs
Is the breathing of the dead.
Those who are dead have never gone away.
They are in the shadows darkening around,
They are in the shadows fading into day,
The dead are not under the ground.
They are in the trees that quiver,
They are in the woods that weep,
They are in the waters of the rivers,
They are in the waters that sleep.
They are in the crowds, they are in the homestead.
The dead are never dead.
Listen more to things
Than to words that are said.
The water's voice sings
And the flame cries
And the wind that brings
The woods to sighs
Is the breathing of the dead.
Who have not gone away
Who are not under the ground
Who are never dead.
Those who are dead have never gone away.
They are at the breast of the wife.

They are in the child's cry of dismay
And the firebrand bursting into life.
The dead are not under the ground.
They are in the fire that burns low
They are in the grass with tears to shed,
In the rock where whining winds blow
They are in the forest, they are in the homestead.
The dead are never dead.
Listen more to things
Than to words that are said.
The water's voice sings
And the flame cries
And the wind that brings
The woods to sighs
Is the breathing of the dead.
And repeats each day
The Covenant where it is said
That our fate is bound to the law,
And the fate of the dead who are not dead
To the spirits of breath who are stronger than they.
We are bound to Life by this harsh law
And by this Covenant we are bound
To the deeds of the breathings that die
Along the bed and the banks of the river,
To the deeds of the breaths that quiver
In the rock that whines and the grasses that cry
To the deeds of the breathings that lie
In the shadow that lightens and grows deep
In the tree that shudders, in the woods that weep,
In the waters that flow and the waters that sleep,
To the spirits of breath which are stronger than they
That have taken the breath of the deathless dead
Of the dead who have never gone away

Of the dead who are not now under the ground.
Listen more to things
Than to words that are said.
The water' voice sings
And the flame cries
And the wind that brings
The woods to sighs
Is the breathing of the dead.

JOHN PEPPER CLARK(1935-2020)

John Pepper Clark was born in Kiagbodo, in Nigeria. He was a poet, and playwright. He had his early education in Native Authority School, Okrika and later in the prestigious Government College in Ughelli. He studied in the University of Abadan and taught in the university of Logos. He worked in the Ministry of Information and Broadcasting. His main collections of poems are- *Poems*(1961), A *Reed in the Tide* (1965) and *Casualties:Poems1966-68*.

92. The Causalities to Chinua Achebe

The casualties are not only those who are dead.
They are well out of it.
The casualties are not only those who are dead.
Though they await burial by installment.
The casualties are not only those who are lost
Persons or property, hard as it is
To grope for a touch that some
May not know is not there.
The casualties are not only those led away by night.
The cell is a cruel place, sometimes a haven.
Nowhere as absolute as the grave.
The casualties are not only those who started
A fire and now cannot put out, Thousands
Are are burning that have no say in the matter.
The casualties are not only those who are escaping.
The shattered shall become prisoners in
A fortress of falling walls
The casualties are many, and a good member as well
Outside the scenes of ravage and wreck;
They are the emissaries of rift,
So smug in smoke -rooms they haunt abroad,
They do not see the funeral piles
At home eating up the forests.
They are wandering minstrels who, beating on
The drums of the human heart, draw the world
Into a dance with rites it does not know.
The drums overwhelm the guns...
Caught in the clash of counter claims and charges
How Can I Go On When not in the niche others left,

We fall.
All casualties of the war.
Because we cannot hear each other speak.
Because eyes have ceased the face from the crowd.
Because whether we know or
Do not the extent of wrongs on all sides,
We are characters now other than before
The war began, the stay-at-home unsettled
By taxes and rumours, the looters for office
And wares, fearful everyday the owners may return.
We are all casualties,
All sagging as are
The cases celebrated for kwashiorkor.
The unforseen camp - follower of not just our war.

93. Olokun

I love to pass my fingers
(As tide thro' weeds of the sea
And wind the tall fern-fronds)
Thro' the strands of your hair
Dark as night that screens the naked moon:
I am jealous and passionate
Like Jehovah, God of the Jews,
And I would that you realise
No greater love had woman
From man than the one I have for you!
But what wakeful eyes of man,
Made of the mud of this earth,
Can stare at the touch of sleep
The sable vehicle of dream
Which indeed is the look of your eyes!
So drunken, like ancient walls
We crumble in heaps at your feet;
And as the good maid of the sea,
Full of rich bounties for men,
You lift us all beggars to your breast.

94. Night Rain

What time of night it is
I do not know
Except that like some fish
Doped out of the deep
I have bobbed up bellywise
From stream of sleep
And no cocks crow.
It is drumming hard here
And I suppose everywhere
Droning with insistent ardour upon
Our roof thatch and shed
And thro' sheaves slit open
To lightning and rafters
I cannot quite make out overhead
Great water drops are dribbling
Falling like orange or mango
Fruits showered forth in the wind
Or perhaps I should say so
Much like beads I could in prayer tell
Them on string as they break
In wooden bowls and earthenware
Mother is busy now deploying
About our roomlet and floor.
Although it is so dark
I know her practiced step as
She moves her bins, bags and vats
Out of the run of water
That like ants gain possession
Of the floor. Do not tremble then

But turns, brothers, turn upon your side
Of the loosening mats
To where the others lie.
We have drunk tonight of a spell
Deeper than the owl's or hat's
That wet of wings may not fly
Bedraggled up on the iroko, they stand
Emptied of hearts, and
Therefore will not stir, no, not
Even at dawn for then
They must scurry in to hide.
So let us roll over on our back
And again roll to the beat
Of drumming all over the land
And under its ample soothing hand
Joined to that of the sea
We will settle to sleep of the innocent and free.

WOLE SOYINKA (1934-2010)

Wole Soyinka was born in 1934 in Abeokuta. In 1954 he attended the Government College, Ibadan, and later the University of Leeds, England and he wrote his first play *The Lionand the Jewel.* He is a great Nigerian writer who won the Nobel Prize for literature in 1986. He was poet, playwright, essayist critic and journalist. His poetical collections are- *TelephoneConversation*(1963), *IdanreandOtherPoems*(1967) and *A Shuttle in the Crypt* (1971) etc.

95. Agbor Dancer

See her caught in the throb of a drum
Tippling from hide-brimmed stem
Down lineal veins to ancestral core
Opening out in her supple tan
Limbs like fresh foliage in the sun.
See how entangled in the magic
Maze of music
In trance she treads the intricate
Pattern rippling crest after crest
To meet the green clouds of the forest
Tremulous beats wake trenchant
In her heart a descant
Tingling quick to her finger tips
And toes virginal habits long
Too atrophied for pen or tongue.
Could I, early sequsster's from my tribe,
Free a lead-tether'd scribe
I should answer her communal call
Lose myself in her warm caress
Intervolving earth, sky and flesh.

96. Telephonic Conversation

The price seemed reasonable, location
Indifferent. The landlady swore she lived
Off premises. Nothing remained
But self-confession. 'Madam', I warned,
'I hate a wasted journey—I am—African'.
Silence. Silenced transmission of
Pressurised good-breeding. Voice, when it came,
Lip-stick coated, long gold-rolled
Cigarette-holder pipped. Caught I was, foully.
'HOW DARK?' ... I had not misheard...
ARE YOU LIGHT
OR VERY DARK?' Button B.Button A Stench
Of rancid breath of public-hide-and-speak
Red booth. Red Pillar-box. Red double-tiered
Omnibus squelching tar. It was real! Shamed
By ill-mannered silence, surrender
Pushed dumb foundment to beg simplification.
Considerate she was, varying the emphasis—
'ARE YOU DARK? OR VERY LIGHT?'
Revelation came.
You mean—like plain or milk chocolate?'
Her assent was clinical, crushing in its light
Impersonality. Rapidly, wave-length adjusted,
I chose, 'West African Sepia'—and as an afterthought,
'Down in my passport.' Silence for spectroscopic
Flight of fancy, till truthfulness clanged her accent
Hard on the mouthpiece. 'WHAT'S THAT?' conceding
'DON'T KNOW WHAT THAT IS'. 'Like brunette'.
THAT'S DARK, ISN'T IT?' 'Not altogether.

Facially, I am brunette, but madam, you should see
The rest of me. Palm of my hand, soles of my feet
Are a peroxide blond. Friction, caused—
Foolishly madam—by sitting down, has turned
My bottom raven black—One moment madam '
—sensing
Her receiver rearing on the thunder clap
About my ears—'Madam/ I pleaded, 'Wouldn't
you rather
See for yourself?'.

97. Dedication

Earth will not share the rafter's envy: dung floors
Break, not the gecko's slight skin, but its fall
Taste this soil for death and plumb her deep for life
As this yam, wholly earthed, yet a living tuber
To the warmth of waters, earthed as springs As roots
of baobab, as the hearth.
The air will not deny you. Like a top
Spin you on the navel of the storm, for the hoe
That roots the forests ploughs a path for squirrels.
Be ageless as dark peat, but only that rain's
Fingers, not the feet of men may wash you over.
Long wear the sun's shadow; run naked to the night.
Peppers green and red—child—your tongue arch
To scorpion tail, spit straight return to danger's threats
Yet coo with the brown pigeon, tendril dew between
your lips.
Shield you like the flesh of palms, skyward held
Cuspids in thorn nesting, insealed as the heart of
kernel—
A woman's flesh is oil—child, palm oil on your tongue
Is suppleness to life, and wine of this gourd
From self-same timeless run of runnels as refill
Your podlings, child, weaned from yours we embrace
Earth's honeyed milk, wine of the only rib.
Now roll your tongue in honey till your cheeks are
Swarming honeycombs—Your world needs
sweetening, child.
Camwood round the heart, chalk for flight
Of blemish—see? it dawns!—antimony beneath

Armpits like a goddess, and leave this taste
Long on your lips, of salt, that you may seek
None from tears. This, rain-water, is the gift of gods—
drink of its purity, bear fruits in season.
Fruits then to your lips; haste to repay
The debt of birth. Yield man-tides like the sea
And ebbing, leave a meaning on the fossilled sands.

98. To my First White Hairs

Hirsute hell chimney-spouts, black thunderthroes
confluence of coarse cloudfleeces—My head sir!
—scourbrush
in bitumen, past fossil beyond fingers of light—until ...!
Sudden sprung as corn stalk after rain, watered milk weak;
as lightning shrunk to ant's antenna, shrivelled off the
febrile sight of crickets in the sun
—THREE WHITE HAIRS! frail invaders of the
undergrowth
interpret time. I view them, wired wisps, vibrant coiled
beneath a magnifying glass, milk-thread presages
Of the hoary phase. Weave then, weave o quickly weave
your sham veneration. Knit me webs of winter sagehood,
nightcap and the fungoid sequins of a crown.

99. Fado Singer: For Amalia Roderiguez

My skin is pumiced to a fault
I am down to hair-roots, down to fibre filters
Of the raw tobacco nerve
Your net is spun of sitar strings
To hold the griefs of gods: I wander long
In tear vaults of the sublime
Queen of night torments, you strain
Sutures of song to bear imposition of the rites
Of living and death. You
Pluck strange dirges from the storm
Sift rare stones from ashes of the moon, and rise
Night errands to the throne of anguish
Oh there is too much crush of petals
For perfume, too heavy tread of air on moth-wing
For a cup of rainbow dust
Too much pain, oh midwife at the cry
Of severance, fingers at the cosmic cord, too vast
The pains of easters for a hint of the eternal
I would be free of your tyranny, free
From sudden plunges of the flesh in earthquake
Beyond all subsidence of sense
I would be free from headlong rides
In rock reams and volcanic veins, drawn by dark steeds
On grey melodic reins.

DAVID DIOP (1927-1960)

He was a French West African poet known for his fine poetry of Negritude. As a school boy he wrote poems and published in *PresenceAfricaine*. His work reflects his anti- colonial stance. His small collection of poems is *Coups de pion*. Unfortunately he died in an air crash in 1960.

100. Africa

Africa my Africa
Africa of proud warriors in ancestral Savannahs
Africa of whom my grandmother sings
On the banks of the distant river
I have never known you
But your blood flows in my veins
Your beautiful black blood that irrigates the fields
The blood of your sweat
The sweat of your work
The work of your slavery
Africa, tell me Africa
Is this your back that is unbent
This back that never breaks under the weight of humiliation
This back trembling with red scars
And saying no to the whip under the midday sun?
But a grave voice answers me
Impetuous child that tree, young and strong
That tree over there
Splendidly alone amidst white and faded flowers
That is your Africa springing up anew
springing up patiently, obstinately
Whose fruit bit by bit acquires
The bitter taste of liberty.

STANDISH O GRANDY
(1793-1846)

He was an Irish Canadian poet and priest.

101. Winter in Lower Canada

Thou barren waste; unprofitable strand,
Where hemlocks brood on unproductive land,
Whose frozen air on one bleak winter's night
Can metamorphose dark brown hares to white!
Here forests crowd, unprofitable lumber,
O'er fruitless lands indefinite as number;
Where birds scarce light, and with the north winds veer
On wings of wind, and quickly disappear,
Here the rough Bear subsists his winter year,
And one sound policy conduct the whole.

ALEXANDER McLACHLAN (1818-1896)

He was born in Johnstone, United Kingdom. He was a Scottish born Canadian poet and priest. Also he was a farmer and tailor and emigrant agent. And he was very active in the mid-nineteenth century and wrote both in Scottish dialect and poetic convention of sickness of Scottish immigrants to Canada. His collections of poems are- *Poems*(1846), *SpiritofLoveadOther Poems*(1846), *Lyrics*(1858), *TheEmigrantandOther Poems*(1961).

102. Song

Old England is eaten by knaves,
Yet her heart is all right at the core,
May she ne'er be the mother of slaves,
Nor a foreign foe land on her shore.
I love my own country and race,
Nor lightly I fled from them both,
Yet who would remain in a place
Where there's too many spoons for the broth.
The squire's preserving his game.
He says that God gave it to him,
And he'll banish the poor without shame,
For touching a feather or limb.
The Justice he feels very big,
And boasts what the law can secure,
But has two different laws in his wig,
Which he keeps for the rich and the poor.
The Bishop he preaches and prays,
And talks of a heavenly birth,
Bur somehow, for all that he says,
He grabs a good share of the earth.
Old England is eaten by knaves,
Yet her heart is all right at the core,
May she ne'er be the mother of slaves,
Nor a foreign foe land on her shore.

CHARLES SANGSTER
(1822-1893)

He was one of early Canadian poets. He was born in Kingston, Canada, and died there. He was son of Anne Ross and James Sangster. At 15 he left the school to help provide for the family. He worked in the naval industry, making cartridges. He wrote his first 700 line poem under the title "The Rebel" in 1839. His other work is *TheStLawrenceandthe Saguenayand Other Poems*. In 1882, He was elected as fellow of the Royal Society of Canada.

103. The Thousand Islands

The bark leaps love-fraught from the land; the sea
Lies calm before us. Many an isle is there,
Clad with soft verdure; many a stately tree
Uplifts its leafy branches through the air;
The amorous current bathes the islets fair,
As we skip, youth-like, o'er the limpid waves;
White cloudlets speck the golden atmosphere,
Through which the passionate sun looks down, and graves
His image on the pearls that boil from the deep caves,
And bathe the vessel's prow. Isle after isle
Is passed, as we glide tortuously through
The opening vistas, that uprise and smile
Upon us from the ever-changing view.
Here nature, lavish of her wealth, did strew
Her flocks of panting islets on the breast
Of the admiring River, where they grew,
Like shapes of Beauty, formed to give a zest
To the charmed mind, like waking Visions of the Blest.
The silver-sinewed arms of the proud Lake,
Love-wild, embrace each islet tenderly,
The zephyrs kiss the flowers when they wake
At morn, flushed with a rare simplicity;
See how they bloom around yon birchen tree,
And smile along the bank, by the sandy shore,
In lovely groups — a fair community!
The embossed rocks glitter like golden ore,
And here, the o'erarching trees form a fantastic bower.
Red walls of granite rise on either hand,
Rugged and smooth; a proud young eagle soars

Above the stately evergreens, that stand
Like watchful sentinels on these God-built towers;
And near yon beds of many-colored flowers
Browse two majestic deer, and at their side
A spotted fawn all innocently cowers;
In the rank brushwood it attempts to hide,
While the strong-antlered stag steps forth with lordly stride,
And slakes his thirst, undaunted, at the stream.
Isles of o'erwhelming beauty! surely here
The wild enthusiast might live, and dream
His life away. No Nymphic trains appear,
To charm the pale Ideal Worshipper
Of Beauty; nor Neriads from the deeps below;
Nor hideous Gnomes, to fill the breast with fear:
But crystal streams through endless landscapes flow,
And o'er the clustering Isles the softest breezes blow.

...

And now 'tis Night. A myriad stars have come
To cheer the earth, and sentinel the skies.
The full-orbed moon irradiates the gloom,
And fills the air with light. Each Islet lies
Immersed in shadow, soft as thy dark eyes;
Swift through the sinuous path our vessel glides,
Now hidden by the massive promontories,
Anon the bubbling silver from its sides
Spurning, like a wild bird, whose home is on the tides.
Here Nature holds her Carnival of Isles.
Steeped in warm sunlight all the merry day,
Each nodding tree and floating greenwood smiles,
And moss-crowned monsters move in grim array;
All night the Fisher spears his finny prey;
The piney flambeaux reddening the deep,
Past the dim shores, or up some mimic bay:

Like grotesque banditti they boldly sweep
Upon the startled prey, and stab them while they sleep.
Many a tale of legendary lore
Is told of these romantic Isles. The feet
Of the Red Man have pressed each wave-zoned shore,
And many an eye of beauty oft did greet
The painted warriors and their birchen fleet,
As they returned with trophies of the slain.
That race has passed away; their fair retreat
In its primeval loneness smiles again,
Save where some vessel snaps the isle-enwoven chain:
Save where the echo of the huntsman's gun
Startles the wild duck from some shallow nook,
Or the swift hounds' deep baying, as they run,
Rouses the lounging student from his book;
Or where, assembled by some sedgy brook,
A pic-nic party, resting in the shade,
Spring pleasedly to their feet, to catch a look
At the strong steamer, through the watery glade
Ploughing, like a huge serpent from its ambuscade.

CHARLES MAIR (1838-1927)

He was born in Lanark, Canada in 1838. He was educated in the Queen's University. He was a poet, journalist and social and political activist. He participated in the first Canadian movement and also in Rein Rebellion as an officer in 1885. His poetical works are- *Dreamland and Other Poems* (1868) and *Tecumseh*(1886). He died in Victoria, Canada.

104. From Tecumseh(i)

There was a time on this fair continent
When all things throve in spacious peacefulness.
The prosperous forests unmolested stood,
For where the stalwart oak grew there it lived
Long ages, and then died among its kind.
The hoary pines—those ancients of the earth—
Brimful of legends of the early world,
Stood thick on their own mountains unsubdued.
And all things else illumined by the sun,
Inland or by the lifted wave, had rest.
The passionate or calm pageants of the skies
No artist drew; but in the auburn west
Innumerable faces of fair cloud
Vanished in silent darkness with the day.
The prairie realm—vast ocean's paraphrase
Rich in wild grasses numberless, and flowers
Unnamed save in mute Nature's inventory,
No civilized barbarian trenched for gain.
And all that flowed was sweet and uncorrupt
The rivers and their tributary streams,
Undammed, wound on forever, and gave up
Their lonely torrents to weird gulfs of sea,
And ocean wastes unshadowed by a sail.
And all the wild life of this western world
Knew not the fear of man; yet in those woods,
And by those plenteous streams and mighty lakes,
And on stupendous steppes of peerless plain,
And in the rocky gloom of canyons deep,
Screened by the stony ribs of mountains hoar

Which steeped their snowy peaks in purging cloud,
And down the continent where tropic suns
Warmed to her very heart the mother earth,
And in the congcal'd north where silence self
Ached with intensity of stubborn frost,
There lived a soul more wild than barbarous;
A tameless soul—the sunburnt savage free—
Free, and untainted by the greed of gain:
Great Nature's man content with Nature's food.
LEFROY. I love you better than I love my race;
And could I mass my fondness for my friends,
Augment it with my love of noble brutes,
Tap every spring of reverence and respect,
And all affections bright and beautiful—
Still would my love for you outweigh them all.
IENA. Speak not of love! Speak of the Long-Knife's hate!
Oh, it is pitiful to creep in fear
O'er lands where once our fathers stept in pride!
The Long-Knife strengthens, whilst our race decays,
And falls before him as our forests fall.
First comes his pioneer, the bee, and soon
The mast which plumped the wild deer fats his swine.
His cattle pasture where the bison fed;
His flowers, his very weeds, displace our own—
Aggressive as himself. All, all thrust back!
Destruction follows us, and swift decay.
Oh, I have lain for hours upon the grass,
And gazed into the tenderest blue of heaven—
Cleansed as with dew, so limpid, pure and sweet—
All flecked with silver packs of standing cloud
Most beautiful! But watch them narrowly!
Those clouds will sheer small fleeces from their sides,
Which, melting in our sight as in a dream,

Will vanish all like phantoms in the sky.
So melts our heedless race! Some weaned away,
And wedded to rough-handed pioneers,
Who, fierce as wolves in hatred of our kind,
Yet from their shrill and acid women turn,
Prizing our maidens for their gentleness.
Some by outlandish fevers die, and some—
Caught in the white man's toils and vices mean—
Court death, and find it in the trader's cup.
And all are driven from their heritage,
Far from our fathers' seats and sepulchres,
And girdled with the growing glooms of war;
Resting a moment here, a moment there,
Whilst ever through our plains and forest realms
Bursts the pale spoiler, armed, with eager quest,
And ruinous lust of land. I think of all—
And own Tecumseh right. 'Tis he alone
Can stem this tide of sorrows dark and deep;
So must I bend my feeble will to his,
And, for my people's welfare, banish love.

GEORGE FREDERICK CAMERON (1854-1885)

He was a Canadian poet, lawyer and journalist best known for the liberetto poems. He was born in New Glasgow, Nova Scottia and educated there. He graduated in law from the Boston University of Law in 1877. He is considered one of the Confederation Poets. His famous poem, "On Leaving the Coast of Nova Scottia" was anthologized in *Songs of the Great Dominion*. Personally and in collaboration, he edited several books of poems.

105. The Future

O POET of the future! I,
Of the dead Present, bid thee hail!
Come forth and speak,—our speech shall die:
Come forth and sing,—our song shall fail:
Our speech, our song fall barren,—we go by!
Our heart is weak. In vain it swells
And beats to bursting at the wrong:
There never sets a sun but tells
Of weak ones trampled down by strong,
Of Truth and Justice both immured in cells.
We would aspire, but round us lies
A maze of high desires and aims;
Would seek a prize, but, ah! our eyes
Fail as we face the fallen fames
Of the great world's Olympian games.
Seeing the victors vanquished, we
Grow heartsick at the sight, and choose
To hold in fee what things there be
Rather than in the hazard use,—
Than stake the all we have—to lose!
We all are feeble. Still we tread
An ever-upward sloping way;
Deep chasms and dark are round us spread
And bale-fires beckon us astray:But thou
shalt stand upon the mountain head.
But thou wilt look with gladdened eyes
And see the mist of error flee,
And see the happy suns arise
Of happier days that are to be,—

On greener, gladder earth, and clearer skies.
We, of the Morning, but behold
The dawn afar: thine eye shalt see
The full and perfect day unfold,—
The full and perfect day to be,
When Justice shall return as lovely as of old.
Thou, with unloosened tongue,
shalt speak In words of subtle, silver sound,—
In words not futile now, nor weak,
To all the nations listening round
Until they seek the light,—nor vainly seek!
We only ask it as our share,
That, when your day-star rises clear,—
A perfect splendour in the air,—
A glory ever, far and near,—
Ye write such words—
as these of those who were!

SIR CHARLES G.D.ROBERTS
(1860-1944)

He was born in Douglas, News Brunswick. He was mostly homeschooled by his father. He was raised in the parish of Westcock, New Brunswick. He attended Fredericton Collegiate School for two years and then he moved to the University of New Brunswick and did his M.A. in1881. His main works are- *SongsoftheCommon Day* (1893), *TheBookofthe Rose*(1903), and *TheIcebergand Other Poems*(1934).

106. The Solitary Woodsman

When the grey lake-water rushes
Past the dripping alder-bushes,
And the bodeful autumn wind
In the fir-tree weeps and hushes, —
When the air is sharply damp
Round the solitary camp,
And the moose-bush in the thicket
Glimmers like a scarlet lamp, —
When the birches twinkle yellow,
And the cornel bunches mellow,
And the owl across the twilight
Trumpets to his downy fellow, —
When the nut-fed chipmunks romp
Through the maples' crimson pomp,
And the slim viburnum flushes
In the darkness of the swamp, —
When the blueberries are dead,
When the rowan clusters red,
And the shy bear, summer-sleekened,
In the bracken makes his bed, —
On a day there comes once more
To the latched and lonely door,
Down the wood-road striding silent,
One who has been here before.
Green spruce branches for his head,
Here he makes his simple bed,
Crouching with the sun, and rising
When the dawn is frosty red.
All day long he wanders wide

With the grey moss for his guide,
And his lonely axe-stroke startles
The expectant forest-side.
Toward the quiet close of day
Back to camp he takes his way,
And about his sober footsteps
Unafraid the squirrels play.
On his roof the red leaf falls,
At his door the bluejay calls,
And he hears the wood-mice hurry
Up and down his rough log walls;
Hears the laughter of the loon
Thrill the dying afternoon;
Hears the calling of the moose
Echo to the early moon.
And he hears the partridge drumming,
The belated hornet humming, —
All the faint, prophetic sounds
That foretell the winter's coming.
And the wind about his eaves
Through the chilly night-wet grieves,
And the earth's dumb patience fills him,
Fellow to the falling leaves.

WILFRED CAMPBELL
(1861-1918)

He was a Canadian 'Confederation' poet, clergyman, writer, and civil servant. Born in Berlin, NewMarket, Ontario. His father was Church Of England clergyman. He attend his native High school and taught before entering the University of Toronto, University College, 1880. He became a strong advocate of British imperialism during the 20th century, His main poetical works are- *Poems 1879-1880, Lake Lyrics and Other Poems* (2016) and *TheDreadVoyage: Poems*(2016).

107. The Winter Lakes

Out in a world of death far to the northward lying,
Under the sun and the moon, under the dusk and the day;
Under the glimmer of stars and the purple of sunsets dying,
Wan and waste and white, stretch the great lakes away.
Never a bud of spring, never a laugh of summer,
Never a dream of love, never a song of bird;
But only the silence and white, the shores that grow
chiller and dumber,
Wherever the ice winds sob, and the griefs of winter are
heard.
Crags that are black and wet out of the grey lake looming,
Under the sunset's flush and the pallid, faint glimmer of
dawn;
Shadowy, ghost-like shores, where midnight surfs are booming
Thunders of wintry woe over the spaces wan.
Lands that loom like spectres, whited regions of winter,
Wastes of desolate woods, deserts of water and shore;
A world of winter and death, within these regions who enter,
Lost to summer and life, go to return no more.
Moons that glimmer above, waters that lie white under,
Miles and miles of lake far out under the night;
Foaming crests of waves, surfs that shoreward thunder,
Shadowy shapes that flee, haunting the spaces white.
Lonely hidden bays, moon-lit, ice-rimmed, winding,
Fringed by forests and crags, haunted by shadowy shores;
Hushed from the outward strife, where the mighty surf
is grinding
Death and hate on the rocks, as sandward and landward
it roars.

ARCHIBALD LAMPMAN (1861-1999) FRSC

He was born in Morpeth, Ontario, a village, near Chattam. He was the son of an Anglican clergyman. He attended Barron's school, In 1868 he contracted rheumatic fever and developed permanently a weak heart. He also studied in Cobourg Collegiate and Trinity College school, Port hope, Ontario. His main collection of poems is- *Amongthe MilletandOtherPoems*(1888), *LyricsoftheEarth*(1895) and Duncan Scott Campbell edited his *AttheLongSaultandOther Poems*in 1943.

108. The City of the End of Things

Beside the pounding cataracts
Of midnight streams unknown to us
'Tis builded in the leafless tracts
And valleys huge of Tartarus.
Lurid and lofty and vast it seems;
It hath no rounded name that rings,
But I have heard it called in dreams
The City of the End of Things.
Its roofs and iron towers have grown
None knoweth how high within the night,
But in its murky streets far down
A flaming terrible and bright
Shakes all the stalking shadows there,
Across the walls, across the floors,
And shifts upon the upper air
From out a thousand furnace doors;
And all the while an awful sound
Keeps roaring on continually,
And crashes in the ceaseless round
Of a gigantic harmony.
Through its grim depths re-echoing
And all its weary height of walls,
With measured roar and iron ring,
The inhuman music lifts and falls.
Where no thing rests and no man is,
And only fire and night hold sway;
The beat, the thunder and the hiss
Cease not, and change not, night nor day.
And moving at unheard commands,

The abysses and vast fires between,
Flit figures that with clanking hands
Obey a hideous routine;
They are not flesh, they are not bone,
They see not with the human eye,
And from their iron lips is blown
A dreadful and monotonous cry;
And whoso of our mortal race
Should find that city unaware,
Lean Death would smite him face to face,
And blanch him with its venomed air:
Or caught by the terrific spell,
Each thread of memory snapt and cut,
His soul would shrivel and its shell
Go rattling like an empty nut.
It was not always so, but once,
In days that no man thinks upon,
Fair voices echoed from its stones,
The light above it leaped and shone:
Once there were multitudes of men,
That built that city in their pride,
Until its might was made, and then
They withered age by age and died.
But now of that prodigious race,
Three only in an iron tower,
Set like carved idols face to face,
Remain the masters of its power;
And at the city gate a fourth,
Gigantic and with dreadful eyes,
Sits looking toward the lightless north,
Beyond the reach of memories;
Fast rooted to the lurid floor,
A bulk that never moves a jot,

In his pale body dwells no more,
Or mind or soul,—an idiot!
But sometime in the end those three
Shall perish and their hands be still,
And with the master's touch shall flee
Their incommunicable skill.
A stillness absolute as death
Along the slacking wheels shall lie,
And, flagging at a single breath,
The fires shall moulder out and die.
The roar shall vanish at its height,
And over that tremendous town
The silence of eternal night
Shall gather close and settle down.
All its grim grandeur, tower and hall,
Shall be abandoned utterly,
And into rust and dust shall fall
From century to century;
Nor ever living thing shall grow,
Nor trunk of tree, nor blade of grass;
No drop shall fall, no wind shall blow,
Nor sound of any foot shall pass:
Alone of its accursèd state,
One thing the hand of Time shall spare,
For the grim Idiot at the gate
Is deathless and eternal there.

DUNCUN CAMPBELL SCOTT(1862-1947)

He was a poet, civil servant and prose writer. He was born in Ottawa, Ontario. He was the son of the Rev William Scott, a Methodist preacher. He was educated in Stanstead Wesleyan College. In early life he became an accomplished pianist. His main collection of poems are- *The Magic House and Other Poems*(1893), *Labourand Angel* (1898) and *Lundy'sLane andOtherPoems*(1916).

109. A Prairie Water Colour

In double lines of silver-grey: —
A trembling in the silver trees
A shadow-trembling in the slew.
Standing clear above the hill
The snow-grey clouds are still,
Floating there idle as light;
Beyond, the sky is almost white
Under the pure deep zenith-blue.
Acres of summer-fallow meet
Acres of growing gold-green wheat
That ripen in the heat.
Where a disc-harrow tears the soil,
Up the long slope six horses toil,
The driver, one with the machine; —
The group is dimly seen
For as they go a cloud of dust
Comes like a spirit out of earth
And follows where they go.
Upward they labour, drifting slow,
The disc-rims sparkle through the veil;
Now upon the topmost height
The dust grows pale,
The group springs up in vivid light
And, dipping below the line of sight,
Is lost to view.
Yet still the little cloud is there,
All dusky-luminous in air,
Then thins and settles on the land
And lets the sunlight through.

All is content. The fallow field
Is waiting there till next year's yield
Shall top the rise with ripening grain,
When the green-gold harvest plain
Shall break beneath the harrow.
Still-purple, growing-gold they lie,
The crop and summer fallow. The vast sky
Holds all in one pure round of blue —
And nothing moves except the play
Of silver-grey in the poplar trees
Of shadow in the slew.

W. W. E. ROSS (1894-1966)

He was a Canadian geophysicist and poet. He was the first to write imagist poetry, surrealistic verse and considered as one of the modern poets of Canada. He was the son of Ralph and Ella Louise Ross. He grew Pembroke, Ontario. He studied in the University of Toronto. He served as geophysicist till his retirement and made surveys in Northern Ontaria. His main collections of poems are- *Laconics*(1930), *Sonnets* (1932), and *Experiment1923-1929*in 1956.

110. The Snake Trying

The snake trying
To escape the pursuing stick,
With sudden curvings of thin
Long body. How beautiful
And graceful are his shapes!
He glides through the water away
From the stroke. O let him go
Over the water
Into the reeds to hid
Without hurt. Small and green
He is harmless even to children.
Along the sand
He lay until observed
And chased away, and now
'He vanishes in the ripples
Among the green slim reeds.'

F. R. SCOTT (1899-1985)

He was also known as Frank Scott. He was a lawyer, poet, and constitutional scholar. He helped to found the first Canadian Social Democratic Party. Born in Quebec city, as the sixth of seven children. His father was an Anglican priest minor poet and advocate of British imperialism. He first studied at Bishop's University, Lennoxville, Quebec, and later he as a Rhodes Scholar attended Magdalen College, Oxford. His collections of poems are- *Overture* (1945), *Events and Signals* (1954), and *Selected Poems*(1966).

111. Laurentian Shield

Hidden in wonder and snow, or sudden with summer,
This land stares at the sun in a huge silence
Endlessly repeating something we cannot hear.
Inarticulate, arctic,
Not written on by history, empty as paper,
It leans away from the world with songs in its lakes
Older than love, and lost in the miles.
This waiting is wanting.
It will choose its language
When it has chosen its technic,
A tongue to shape the vowels of its productivity.
A language of flesh and of roses.
Now there are pre-words,
Cabin syllables,
Nouns of settlement
Slowly forming, with steel syntax,
The long sentence of its exploitation.
The first cry was the hunter, hungry for fur,
And the digger for gold, nomad, no-man, a particle;
Then the bold commands of monopoly, big with
machines,
Carving its kingdoms out of the public wealth;
And now the drone of the plane, scouting the ice,
Fills all the emptiness with neighborhood
And links our future over the vanished pole.
But a deeper note is sounding, heard in the mines,
The scattered camps and the mills, a language of life,
And what will be written in the full culture of occupation
Will come, presently, tomorrow,

From millions whose hands can turn this rock into
children.

ROBERT FINCH (1900-1995)

He was also called as Robert Duer Claydon Finch. Twice he got the Canada's highest literary award, The Governor General'sAward, for poetry. Born in Freeport, Long Island, New York. Educated at the University of Toronto and Sorbonne. He was a professor for French and an expert in French poetry. In 1936 he was a Professor of French (1928-1868). His published 11 poems in *New Provinces*. His collections are- *Poems* (1946), *TheStrengthoftheHills*(1948), and *DoverBeachRevisitedand Other Poems*(1961).

112. Egg and Dart

This never-ended searching for the eyes
Wherein the unasked question's answer lies;
This beating, beating, beating of the heart
Because a contour seems to fit the part;
The long, drear moment of the look that spoils
The little bud of hope; the word that soils
The pact immaculate, so newly born;
The noisy silence of the old self-scorn;
These, and the sudden leaving in the lurch;
Then the droll recommencement of the search.

113. Peacock and Nightingale

Look at the eyes look from my tail!
What other eyes could look so well?
A peacock asks a nightingale.
And how my feathers twist the sun!
Confess that no one, no, no one
Has ever seen such colour spun.
Who would not fall in ecstasy
Before the gemmed enamelry
Of ruby-topaz-sapphire me?
When my proud tail parades its fan,
You, little bird, are merely an
Anachronism in its van.
Let me advise that you be wise,
Avoid the vision of my eyes.
And then the nightingale replies.

A. J. M. SMITH(1902-1980) FRSC

He was a Canadian poet and anthologist. He was a prominent member of the group of Montreal poets. He was born in Montreal but he lived in England for two years. He studied in McGill University and University of Edinburgh. As a graduate he wrote poems and published and co-edited McGill Fortnightly Review. His main collections of poems are- *TheNewsof the Phoenix and Other Poems*(1943) and *A Sort of Ecstasy*(1954) and *CollectedPoems*(1962). He was elected Fellow of the Royal Society of Canada.

114. Ode on the Death of William Butler Yeats

An old thorn tree in a stony place
Where the mountain stream has run dry,
Torn in the black wind under the race
Of the icicle-sharp kaleidoscopic white sky,
Bursts into sudden flower.
Under the central dome of winter and night
A wild swan spreads his fanatic wing.
Ancestralled energy of blood and power
Beats in his sinewy breast. And now the ravening
Soul, fulfilled, his first-last hour
Upon him, chooses to exult.
Over the edge of shivering Europe,
Over the chalk front of Kent, over Eire,
Dwarfing the crawling waves' amoral savagery,
Daring the hiding clouds' rhetorical tumult,
The white swan plummets the mountain top.
The stream has suddenly pushed the papery leaves!
It digs a rustling channel of clear water
On the scarred flank of Ben Bulben.
The twisted tree is incandescent with flowers.
The swan leaps singing into the cold air:
This is a glory not for an hour.
Over the Galway shore
The white bird is flying
Forever, and crying
To the tumultuous throng
Of the sky his cold and passionate song.

115. Like an Old Proud King in a Parable

A bitter king in anger to be gone
From fawning courtier and doting queen
Flung hollow sceptre and gilt crown away,
And breaking bound of all his counties green
He made a meadow in the northern stone
And breathed a palace of inviolable air
To cage a heart that carolled like a swan,
And slept alone, immaculate and gay,
With only his pride for a paramour.
O who is that bitter king? It is not I.
Let me, I beseech thee, Father, die
From this fat royal life, and lie
As naked as a bridegroom by his bride,
And let that girl be the cold goddess Pride.
And I will sing to the barren rock
Your difficult, lonely music, heart,
Like an old proud king in a parable.

A. M. KLEIN (1909-1972)

He was a journalist, poet, novelist, short story writer and lawyer. He was born in Ratno, Unkraine but in 1910 he immigrated to Montreal. He has been called as one of the greatest Canadian poets. He published a novella under the title *The Second Scroll*(1951). He studied in McGill University and the Universitie de Montreal. His main collections of poems are- The Rocking Chair and Other Poems(1954) and Poems (1944).

116. Indian Reservation: Caughnawaga

Where are the braves, the faces like autumn fruit,
who stared at the child from the colored frontispiece?
And the monosyllabic chief who spoke with his throat?
Where are the tribes, the feathered bestiaries?-
Rank Aesop's animals erect and red,
with fur on their names to make all live things kin'-
Chief Running Deer, Black Bear, Old Buffalo Head?
Childhood, that wished me Indian, hoped that
one after school I'd leave the classroom chalk,
the varnish smell, the watered dust of the street,
to join the clean outdoors and the Iroquois track.
Childhood, but always, -as on a calendar,-
there stood that chief, with arms akimbo, waiting
the runaway mascot paddling to his shore.
With what strange moccasin stealth that scene is
changed!
With French names, without paint, in overalls,
their bronze, like their nobility expunged,-
the men. Beneath their alimentary shawls
sit like black tents their squaws; while for the tourist's
brown pennies scattered at the old church door,
the ragged papooses jump, and bite the dust.
Their past is sold in a shop; the beaded shoes,
the sweetgrass basket, the curio Indian,
burnt wood, and gaudy cloth, and inch-canoes-
trophies and scalpings for a traveler's den.
Sometimes, it's true. they dance, but for a bribe;

after a deal don the bedraggled feather
and welcome a white mayor to the tribe.
This is a grassy ghetto, and no home.
And these are fauna in a museum kept.
The better hunters have prevailed. The game,
losing its blood, now makes these grounds it crypt.
The animals pale, the shine of the fur is lost,
bleached are their living bones. About them watch
as through a mist, the pious prosperous ghost.

DOROTHY LIVESAY (1909-1996) FRSC

She was Dorothy Katheleen May Livesay. She was a poetess who won the Governor General Award for poetry twice. Born in Winninpeg, Monitoba. Her mother was a poet and journalist and father, the manager of Canadian Press. She graduated from Trinity College, and studied in the university of Toronto, of British Columbia and Sorbonne. She published 25 collections of poems. Of them -*Green Pitcher* (1928) *New Poems*(1955) and *Collected Poems* (1972) are widely known. She was elected as a Fellow of the Royal Society of Canada.

117. On Looking into Henry Moore

I

Sun stun me sustain me
turn me to stone:
Stone goad me gall me
urge me to run.
When I have found
passivity in fire
and fire in stone
female and male
I'll rise alone
self-extending and self-known.

II

The message of the tree is this
Aloneness is the only bliss
Self-adoration is not in it
(Narcissus tried, but could not win it)
Rather, to extend the root
Tombwards, be at home with death
But in the upper branches know
A green eternity of fire and snow.

III

The fire in the fathest hi8lls
Is where I'd burn myself to bone;
Clad in the armour of the sun
I'd stand a new, alone.
Take off this flesh, this hasty dress
Prepare my half-self my self
One unit, as a tree or stone
Woman in man, and man in womb

P. K. PAGE (1917-2010) FRSC

Patricia Kathleen Page was a British born Canadian poet and was elected as the Fellow of the Royal Society of Canada. Born in Swanage, Dorset, England and moved to Canada in 1919 and alter to Alberta. Her father was an Army Officer. She was a visual artist and exhibited her paintings and works in P.K. Her works are in National Gallery of Canada. Her collections are- *P.K.Page: Poems SelectedandNew*(1974) and *The Golden Lines* (2009).

118. Adolescence

In love they wore themselves in a green embrace.
A silken rain fell through the spring upon them.
In the park she fed the swans and he
whittled nervously with his strange hands.
And white was mixed with all their
colours as if they drew it from the flowering trees.
At night his two finger whistle brought her down
the waterfall stairs to his shy smile
which like an eddy, turned her round and round
lazily and slowly so her will
was nowhere—as in dreams things are and aren't.
Walking along avenues in the dark street lamps sang
like sopranos in their heads with a violence
they never understood and all their
movements when they were together had no conclusion.
Only leaning into the question had they motion;
after they parted were savage and swift as gulls.
asking and asking the hostile emptiness they were
as sharp as partly sculptured stone and all
who watched, forgetting, were amazed to see
them form and fade before their eyes.

119. First Neighbours

In love they wore themselves in a green embrace.
The people I live among, unforgivingly
previous to me, grudging
the way I breathe their
property, the air,
speaking a twisted dialect to my differently
shaped ears
though I tried to adapt
(the girl in a red tattered
petticoat, who jeered at me for my burned bread
Go back where you came from
I tightened my lips; knew that England
was now unreachable, had sunk down into the sea
without ever teaching me about washtubs)
got used to being
a minor invalid, expected to make
inept remarks.
futile and spastic gestures
(asked the Indian
about the squat thing on a stick
drying by the fire: Is that a toad?
Annoyed. he said No no,
deer liver, very good)
Finally I grew a chapped tarpaulin
skin; I negotiated the drizzle
of strange meaning, set it
down to just the latitude:
something to be endured
but not surprised by.

Inaccurate. The forest can still crick me:
one afternoon while I was drawing
birds. a malignant face
flickered over my shoulder;
the branches quivered.
Resolve : to be both tentative and hard to startle
(though clumsiness and
fright are inevitable)
in this area where my damaged
knowing of the language means
prediction is forever impossible.

MARGARET ATWOOD (1939-)
FRSC

Margaret Eleanor Atwood was a poet, novelist, literary critic, teacher, environmentalist and essayist, and inventor. Born in Ottawa, Ontario as the second of three children. She did not go to school but she was a veracious reader. She attended Leaside High School, Leaside and later studied in Victoria College, the University of Toronto and M.A. Radcliffe College of 20 collections of poems *Double Persephone* (1961), *TheAnimalsin that Country* (1968), and *Love Songsofthe Terminator*(1983) are widely known. She was elected for the Royal Society of Canada.

120. Journey to the Interior

In love they wore themselves in a green embrace.
There are similarities
I notice: that the hills
which the eyes make flat as a wall, welded
together, open as I move
to let me through; become
endless as prairies; that the trees
grow spindly, have their roots
often in swamps; that this is a poor country;
that a cliff is not known
as rough except by hand, and is
therefore inaccessible. Mostly
that travel is not the easy going
from point to point, a dotted
line on a map, location
plotted on a square surface
but that I move surrounded by a tangle
of branches, a net of air and alternate
light and dark, at all times;
of branches, a net of air and alternate
light and dark, at all times;
that there are no destinations
apart from this.
There are differences
of course: the lack of reliable charts;
more important, the distraction of small details:
your shoe among the brambles under the chair
where it shouldn't be; lucent
white mushrooms and a paring knife

on the kitchen table; a sentence
crossing my path, sodden as a fallen log
I'm sure I passed yesterday
(have I been
walking in circles again?)
but mostly the danger:
many have been here, but only
some have returned safely.
A compass is useless; also
trying to take directions
from the movements of the sun,
which are erratic;
and words here are as pointless
as calling in a vacant wilderness.
Whatever I do I must
keep my head. I know
it is easier for me to lose my way
forever here, than in other landscapes.

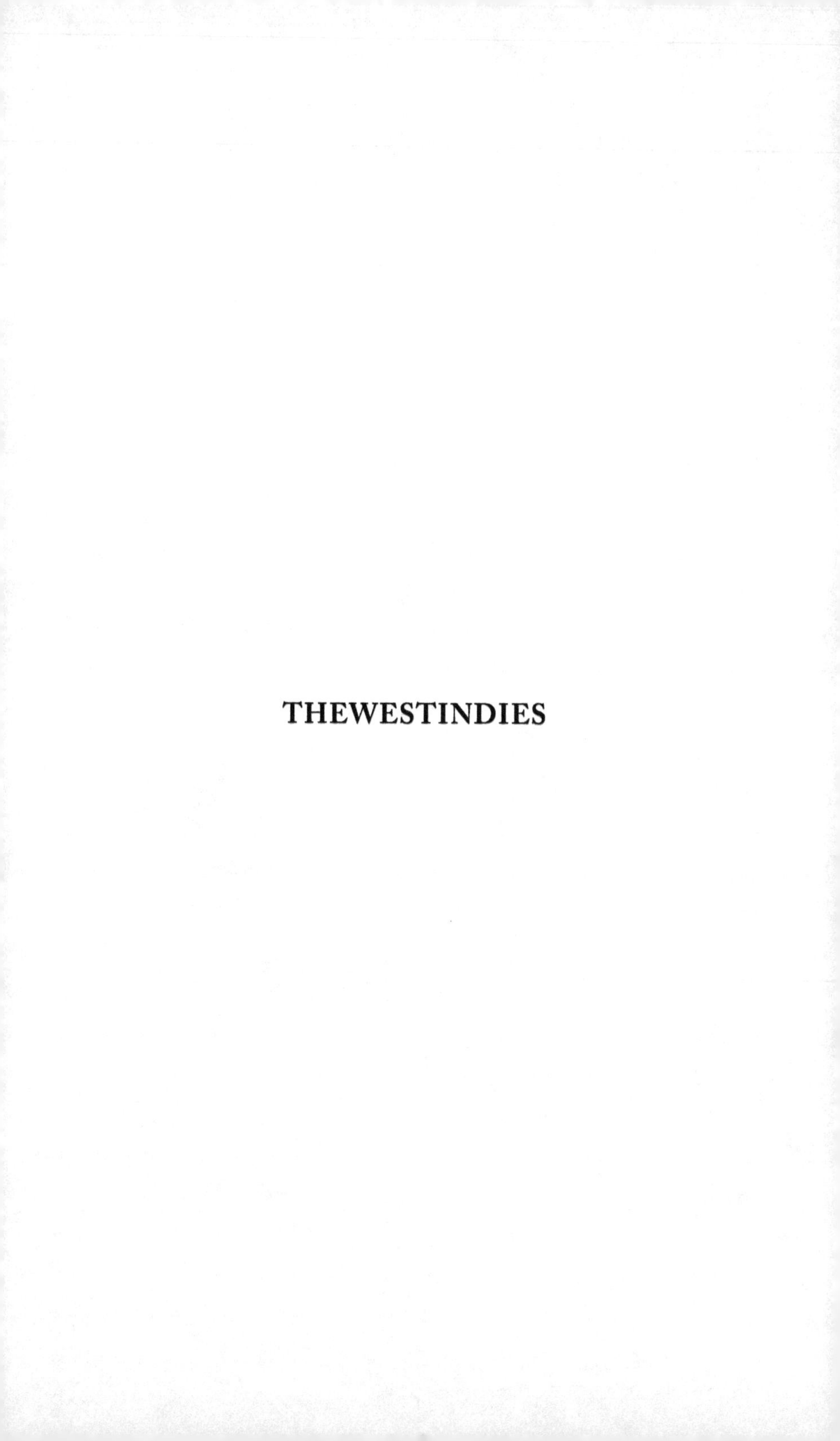

THEWESTINDIES

E.Mc.G. KEANE (1927-1997)

He was a musician and poet, and also worked as jazz trumpeter. He was born on the Caribbean island of St.Vincent and studied in Kingstown Methodist School and he emigrated United Kingdom in 1952. And for some time he worked on the BBC for Caribbean voices. He continued to work as the leader of the jazz band and wrote poetry also. Twice he got married. He moved to Brooklyn. His collections are – *L Oubli* (1950), *Ixion*(1952) *OneWeekwiththe Water*(1978), *Valcano Suite*(1979), and *Palm and Octopus* (1994).

121. The Age of Chains

From Patterns, A Caribbean Sequence
Isn't history amazing?
One time it is gold, or a basket of fish;
Another time it is a woman.
Sometimes it is oil, or perhaps a disagreement
With a Pope.
But mostly it is a stranger on the road to Emmaus.
We recognize it gone.
(God winks for a brief century and a world rots.
One man asked for three days more
and found my world)
Beautiful was my country in time's rains.
Beautiful is my country in the warm hopeful season.
An age of chains did not sully her mountains,
Nor pain's broad knuckle smudge out the sun.
O Beautiful.
I catch her voice in the thick-haired hills,
her impulse. Gathers green in the wood
her breath skying. In the quick tempo of the river
I hear her high singing. A song that is good.
O beautiful.
Up and far beyond care of the wind's corroding,
ruin of star and light's utter end,
toil and her heart's hopes extend
beautiful
Sun's her monument;
and her brightness is of a bright sky's hoarding.
If you see Zaccheus or Balboa
They will define you destiny from a tree.

Drowsing on a cloud I see
A ship bulging westward, with a cargo of groans below...
Commandante Nicolas de Ovando
Enjoyed being Governor of San Domingo
All the Indians worshipped Nicolas
All men admired Nicolas
Except perhaps the priest las Casas
Bartoleme de las Casas, *Apostol de las Indias*
The priest did not like the way Ovando was killing out
the Indians in the cane fields.
Nicolas did not much mind, but he respected priests.
Nicolas did not mean to be cruel
But Spain must be strong, and in any case
You could not leave cane standing in the field forever.
(They say the hurricane waits for the time of ripe cane.)
So when the ships began arriving
And the big black beasts were walked up and down the
decks.
Ovando bought the first boatload for the field.
For this all men admired Nicolas,
Even the priest de las Casas. *Apostol de las Indias*
The new beasts hated Nicolas with a strong black hate.
(O, Hawkins was a sturdy fellow.
White were his teeth as the teeth of the raven.
They buried him in the sea off Puerto Rico).
As near heaven ...
Drowsing on a cloud I watch islands
Soon swarming with black labour.
Life is hot sun and a hot whip
And a more than casual acquaintance with dust.
The old and lucky graduate from
Mud to the master's table
The Big Place.

Some of the masters come down to the warmth
Where the plump girls wait to proffer
Out of fear their dumb efficient embrace.
Africa is lost,
(Hills, O strange woman)
And only a broken syllable records her speech;
(Afrikagodzimiyaba)
Only a granite rhythm redeems her music;
(O flirter with time)
Only in a private whisper, her soul.
Labour now is without dignity'
But the nobility of flesh is not perished.
For in these fields though the slave's
Blood snap and the master weaken his own soul,
Both in the end are martyrs, and bear chains,
The crop's the tyrant. Sugar is king.
And only whip of the ripe cane's blade is soulless.
Africa is not lost.
My fathers sing the sun in one remembered syllable,
And freedom is preserved in private whispers.

EDWARD BRATHWAITE
(1930-2020)

He was a Barbadian poet. Born in Bridgetown, Barbqados to Hilton and Byrl. He had his education in Harrison College, Bridgetown. He had B.A. from Pembroke College. He attended the University of Cambridge. He served as an Education Officer in the Gold Coast with the ministry of Education. Of the 42 collections of poems, only some are known- *Third Word Poems* (1983), *Dream Stories* (194), *Golokwati* (2002) and *Livictus*(2012).

122. Tizzic

For he was a slave
to drums, to flutes, brave
brass and rhythm; the jump-up saved him
from the thought of holes, damp,
rain through the roof of his have-nothing
cottage; kele, kalinda-stamp,
the limbo, calypso-season camp,
these he loved best of all; the road-march tramp
down Princess Street, round Mar-aval; Kitch, Sparrow,
Dougla, these were the stars
of his melodic heaven. Their little winking songs
car-ried him back to days of green unhur-ried growing.
The Car-nival's apotheosis blazed for two nights
without fear or sorrow, colour bar
or anyone to question or restrain his height-ened,
borrowed glory. He walked so far on
stilts of song, of masqueraded story; stars
were near. Doors of St.Peter's heaven were ajar.
Mary, Christ's Christmas mother was there
too, her sweet inclined compassion
in full view. In such bright swinging company
he could no longer feel the cramp
of poverty's confinement, spirit's damp;
he could have all he wished, he ever wanted.
But the good stilts splinter-ed, wood legs broke,
calypso steel pan rhythm faltered.
The midnight church
bell fell across the glow, the lurch-ing cardboard crosses.
Behind the masks, grave

Lenten sorrows waited:
Ash-Wednesday, ashes, darkness, death.
After the *bambalula bambulai*
he was a slave again.

123. So Long, Charlie Parker

For he was a slave
The night before he died
the bird walked on and played
his heart out notes fell
like figure forming pebbles
in a pond . he
was angry . and we
knew he wept to know his time had come
so soon
so little had been done
so little time to do it
in he wished to furl the night from burning
all time long
but time
is short
and life
is short
and breath
is short
and so he
slurred
and slowed
and stopped
his fingers fixed upon a minor
key then slipped
his bright eyes blazed & bulged against the death in him
then
knocking at the door
we watched as one will watch

a great clock striking time from a great booming midnight
bell
the silence slowly throbbing in behind the dying bell

JOHN FIGUERAO (1920-1999)

He is also known as John Joseph Maria Figuerao. He was a poet, teacher, academic, and broadcaster. Born in Kingston, Jamaica to Blanche Maria and Rupert Aston Figuerao. In 1946 he got educated in College of Holy Cross and in the University of London on a BCL scholarship. His main collections of poems are- *BlueMountain Peak* (1944), *Love Leaps Here* (1962), *Ignoring Hurts: Poems*(1976), *The Chase:CollectionofPoems*(1992), *Antonio's World* (1970).

124. On Seeing the Reflection of Notre Dame in the Seine

May 1960
For Louis Arnaud Reid
A man builds better than he knows
The cathedral, stone before flood light's invention,
Through floodlight's shimmering reflection
On matted water long after renews perfection
A man builds better than he knows
What he seeks is not hereafter
But everlasting now well done
The answer in stone or images
Built for the now that is forever
With every invention finds further perfection
He makes the poem, the cathedral
The image, the tune, the stone
So sweetly stretched the tension—
That is perfection—in stone
He cuts stone's dreams, and the world's and his
A man builds better than he knows
A poet at the crossroads
In a strange land,
Caught by his long forgotten song
As it falls from a curtained window,
Suddenly hears it as I see
This night's reflection
Steady in the moving stream
Knowing that he builds well
Who builds better than he knows.

DERECK WALCOTT (1930-2017)

He was a Saint Lucian poet, teacher, journalist, and playwright.He was the son of Alix (Maarlin) and Warwick Walcott. Born and Raised in Castries, Saint Lucia, West Indies. His family was of English, Dutch and African. In 1953 he moved to Trinidad after his graduation. He taught in Boston University and University of Alberta. He was a professor of poetry in the University of Sussex. He wrote nearly 20 collections of poems and plays. He won the Nobel Prize for Literature in 1992. His mist known works are- *Poems* (1951), *The Gulf and Other Poems*(1969), *The Castaway and Other Poems* (1965) and *Selected Poetry* (1981) and *Omeros*, a dramatic epic(1990).

125. Ruins of a Great House

Though our longest sun sets at right
declensions and makes but winter
arches, it cannot be long before we
lie down in darkness, and have our light in ashes...
BROWNE: Urn Burial
Stones only, the *disjecta membra*
of this Great House,
Whose moth-like girls are mixed with candledust,
Remain to file the lizard's dragonish claws;
The months of those gate cherubs streaked with stain.
Axle and coachwheel silted under the muck
Of cattle droppings.
Three crows flap for the trees,
And settle, creaking the eucalyptus boughs.
A smell of dead limes quickens in the nose
The leprosy of Empire.
'Farewell, green fields'
'Farewell, ye happy groves!'
Marble as Greece, like Faulkner's south in stone,
Deciduous beauty prospered and is gone;
But where the lawn breaks in a rash of trees
A spade below dead leaves will ring the bone
Of some dead animal or human thing
Fallen from evil days, from evil times.
It seems that the original crops were limes
Grown in the silt that clogs the river's skirt;
The imperious rakes are gone, their bright girls gone,
The river flows, obliterating hurt.
I climbed a wall with the grill ironwork

Of exiled craftsmen, protecting that great house
From guilt, perhaps, but not from the worm's rent,
Nor from the padded cavalry of the mouse.
And when a wind shook in the limes I heard
What Kipling heard; the death of a great empire,
the abuse Of ignorance by Bible and by sword.
A green lawn, broken by low walls of stone
Dipped to the rivulet, and pacing, I thought next
Of men like Hawkins, Walter Raleigh, Drake,
Ancestral murderers and poets, more perplexed
In memory now by every ulcerous crime.
The world's green age then was a rotting lime
Whose stench became the charnel galleon's text.
The rot remains with us, the men are gone.
But, as dead ash is lifted in a wind,
That fans the blackening ember of the mind,
My eyes burned from the ashen prose of Donne.
Ablaze with rage, I thought
Some slave is rotting in this manorial lake,
And still the coal of my compassion fought:
That Albion too, was once
A colony like ours, Tart of the continent, piece of the main'
Nook-shotten, rook o'er blown, deranged
By foaming channels, and the vain expense
Of bitter faction.
All in compassion ends So differently
from what the heart arranged: 'as well
as if a manor of thy friend's ....'

126. A Sea-Chantey

La, tout n'est au'ordre et beaute,
Luxe, calme, et volupte.
Anguilla, Adina,
Antigua, Cannelles,
Andreuille, all the I's,
Voyelles, of the liquid Antilles,
The names tremble like needles
Of anchored frigates,
Yachts tranquil as lilies,
In ports of calm coral,
The lithe, ebony hulls
Of strait-stitching schooners,
The needles of their masts
That thread archipelagoes
Refracted embroidery
In feverish waters
Of the sea-farer's islands,
Their shorn,leaning palms,
Shaft of Odysseus,
Cyclopic volcanoes,
Creak their own histories,
In the peace of green anchorage;
Flight, and Phyllis,
Returned from the Grenadines,
Names entered this sabbath,
In the port-clerk's register;
Their baptismal names,
The sea's liquid letters,
Repos donnez a cils...

And their blazing cargoes
Of charcoal and oranges;
Quiet, the fury of their ropes.
Daybreak is breaking
On the green chrome water,
The white herons of yachts
Are at sabbath communion,
The histories of schooners
Are murmured in coral,
Their cargoes of sponges
On sandspits of islets
Barques white as white salt
Of acrid Saint Maarten,
Hulls crusted with barnacles,
Holds foul with great turtles,
Whose ship-boys have seen
The blue heave of Leviathan,
A sea-faring, Christian,
And intrepid people.
Now an apprentice washes his cheeks
With sea water and sunlight
In the middle of the harbour
A fish breaks the Sabbath
With a silvery leap.
The scale fall from him
In a tinkle of church-bells;
The town streets are orange
With the week-ripened sunlight,
Balanced on the bowsprit
A young sailor is playing
His grandfather's chantey
On a trembling mouth-organ.
The music curls, dwindling

Like smoke from blue galleys,
To dissolve near the mountains.
The music uncurls with
The soft vowels of inlets.
The christening of vessels,
The titles of portages,
The colours of sea-grapes,
The tartness of sea-almonds,
The alphabet of church-bells,
The peace of white horses
The pastures of ports,
The, litany of islands,
The rosary of archipelagoes,
Anguilla, Antigua,
Virgin of Guadeloupe,
And stone-white
Grenada Of sunlight and pigeons,
The amen of calm waters,
The amen of calm waters,
The amen of calm waters.

127. A Far Cry from Africa

La, tout n'est au'ordre et beaute,
A wind is ruffling the tawny pelt
Of Africa. Kikuyu, quick as flies
Batten upon the bloodstreams of the veldt.
Corpses are scattered through a paradise.
But still the worm, colonel of carrion, cries:
'Waste no compassion on these separate dead'
Statistics justify and scholars seize
The salients of colonial policy.
What is that to the white child hacked in bed?
To savages, expendable as Jews?
Threshed out by beaters, the long rushes break
In a white dust of ibises whose cries
Have wheeled since civilization's dawn
From the parched river or beast-teeming plain;
The violence of beast on beast is read
As natural law, but upright man
Seeks his divinity with inflicting pain.
Delirious as these worried beasts, his wars
Dance to the tightened carcass of a drum,
While he calls courage still, that native dread
Of the white peace contracted by the dead.
Again brutish necessity wipes its hands
Upon the napkin of a dirty cause, again
A waste of our compassion, as with Spain.
The gorilla wrestles with the superman.
I who am poisoned with the blood of both,
Where shall I turn, divided to the vein?
I who have cursed

The drunken officer of British rule, how choose
Between this Africa and the English tongue
I love? Betray them both, or give back what they give?
How can I face such slaughter and be cool?
How can I turn.

EDWARD BAUGH (1936-)

Edward Alston Cecil Baugh, a Jamaican poet and scholar, recognized as authority on the poetry of Dereck Walcott. Born in Port Antonia, Jamiaca.He was the son of Edward Percival Baugh and Ethel Maud. As a student in Titchfield High School he began to write poetry. He studied in the University College of West Indians on a scholarship and later went to Queen's University, Ontario. His main collection is- *Selected Poems*(2007).

128. Elemental

I would have words as tenacious as
mules to bear us, sure-footed up the mountain of night
to where, at daybreak,
we would shake hands with the sun
and breathe the breezes of the farthest ocean
and, as we descended,
in sunlight,
We would be amazed
to see what hazards we had passed.

MERVYN MORRIS (1937-

He was a Jamaican poet and professor emeritus in the University of West Indies, Mona Jamiaca. Born in Kingston, he studied in the University of West indies and as a Rhodes Scholar he went to St. Edmund Hall, Oxford. In 1992 he was a U.K., Arts Council visiting writer- in -residence at the South Bank Centre. His main collections are- *The Pond* (1997), *Shadow Boxing*(1979) and *Examination Centre* (1992).

129. Literary Evening, Jamaica

In a dusty old crumbling building just fit for rats.
And much too large for precious poetry circles
The culture fans sat scattered in the first ten rows
Listening for English poetry.
Geoff read Larkin beautifully, Enright too,
And Michael Saunders talked between the poems:
'I don't say they are wonderful/ he said,
And would not say that anybody says
They're great. I offer them
As two fair English poets writing nowadays.
They're anti-gesture, anti-flatulence,
They speak their quiet honesties without pretence.'
The longer section of the evening's programme
Was poems by the locals, undergraduates,
Some coarse, some wild, and many violent,
All bloody with the strains of rape and childbirth,
Screaming hot curses anti-slavery,
'Down with the limey bastards! Up the blacks!
Chr-rist! Let's tear the painted paper
Off all the blasted cracks!'
The more I heard the more it seemed
A pretty rotten choice to read us Larkin,
Dull-mannered, scared, regressive Phil,
Saying No to everything or Soon, Not yet
So many bulging poets must have blushed
And wondered where the hell they'd ever get
With noisy poems, brash, self-conscious, colourful,
And feared that maybe they were born too crude.
Maybe they were; but it was bloody rude

Seeming to ask for things that don't belong out here
Where sun shines hot and love is plentiful.
For to us standing here, a naked nation
Bracing ourselves for blows, what use
Is tearfulness and bland negation?
What now if honesty should choose
To say, in all this world's confusion
That we are still too young for disillusion?

130. Judas

In a dusty old crumbling building just fit for rats .
That evening, not so long ago, the Master,
fingers in the dish, said gently:
'Did I not choose you twelve,
yet one of you's a devil? 'flocking,
he glanced at me; and others,
quick on cue, looked my way too.
The odd man out is always Judas.
'We're from Galilee' (Nasty little province, smells of fish!)
The point is,
Jesus never trusted me
John, who's favourite, he's from Galilee.
Like Peter, Andrew, all the cosy band.
Which Galilean, Lord, will sit at your right hand?
Tonight I kissed him and I saw
that mocking glance again.
'Betrayest thou the Master
with a kiss?' he said, ironic; then
seemed pleased or something
like relieved he'd got me
right. That knowing judge of men,
he surely ought to realize
that truths are often complicated:
what he spotted he created,
distrusting with those distant
foreign eyes.
The point is not the money. I'll
go give it back. For, hell,
what's thirty bits of silver?

I would not sell
the Master, he's for free. Just
preserve my purity of hate
for him I served and loved so well.
My Lord, the Master of my fate,
always withheld his trust.

STEPHANIE CORREIA
(1930-2000)

She was basically ceramicist and poet and artist, mostly self taught. Her father, originally from Venezuela, was the first Amerindian M.P. She belongs to the country of Guyana. She grew up in Moroccan at Santa Rosa Missin. She wrote several poems and recited them. "Arrows from the Bow"(1988) was the first poem. Her work explored Amerindian life and stories and her imagery drew heavily on Amerindian petroglyphs.

131. Arawak Creation

The Watcher in the Heights looked down
Upon the bare earth with a frown.
He caused the great Kumaka tree
to grow until it touched the sky
And picking twigs and leaves
He threw them down from high.
Those that fluttered turned to birds,
even the little wren, And others touching
earth below became the animals and men.
Fish and other creatures swam in the waters
wild And sitting in the Heights above, the Watcher smiled.

132. Chant to Earth Mother—I

Spirit fighter, sacred rattle—
Fashioned by me from a perfect calabash—
Four mouths to face in all directions,
A crown of brilliant feathers, carrier of crystal fiie
To fight the evil ones, I, only, hold the power
To shake the rattle, chant the song
To use the instruments ancestors left me
To guard, protect and heal the people of my tribe.
Ages ago it seems since first I learnt this lore
Understanding secrets, spirit growing ever stronger,
Bitter years of fasting, self-denial—a child when I began
To walk this testing road, for I am piaiman.
And now true testing time has come
Feathered, fierce-eyed, painted warriors await
My word for a successful hunt.
For first I must go down to underworld
To parley with Earth Mother for the souls of animals
Now gather round, my people help me,
Bear me up with song and dance and ritual
As I embark upon my perilous journey.
Drink the kari, beat the drum, move in sinuous rhythms
Rattle shaking ever faster, tobacco juice, my long cigar;
Ancient incantations rising, falling, chanting endlessly.
Earth shackles break, as I rise up my spirit now set free.
I ride weightlessly upon enchanted bird.
Come guardian helpers lead me through,
Come hawk and eagle, snake and lizard,
Jaguar, alligator, shield me round.
Up steep mountains, through deep lakes

Down long rivers winding dangerous
Through treacherous swamps forests
The demon ones are kept at bay
Until at last deep in the underworld
'Face Earth Mother with my plea
Majestic, threatening, there she stands
Her animals enfolded in her outstretched hand.

SINGAPORE, MALAYSIA AND SRI LANKA

SHIRLY LIM (1944-)

She was born in Malaccan city and raised with her five brothers after her mother abandoned her in childhood. She studied in Infant Jesus Convent and later British Colonial Education System. She did her B.A, with English Literature entering Brandeis University a Waltham. Of nearly fifteen collections of poems two widely known- *Crossing the Peninsula and Other Poems* (1980) *and In Praise of Limes* (2022).

133. Sonnet

No one, I thought loved you so much as I,
Fearful to move abruptly far
If I should lose you. And you, indulgent,
Had undertaken quiet lest I should cry.
No lovers were ever as loyal.
It was sure we knew each other well,
And what we knew we loved, forgetting
Neither the kiss goodnight nor morning.
So consoling, we made disconsolate
Each other; ourselves, to violate;
To shake the unshakeable-seeming firmament
And dance amuck and solitary among the stars.
Now, in tenderness, each to each returned,
We ask, bewildered, where each had gone.

134. Sonnet

I remember clearly child and sea. With time,
both have grown surer.
When, once, listening to water,
She thought to remember the sea,
Precise to the smell, the grain
Of shore and the gathering wave,
The mind worked furious with the grave
Attempt. All senses strained
To hold steady the blue motion
Of looking at.
Where she had been
Then, there is now no recognition.
I see her, the scene of a scene.
Planted, eminent as the sky,
As sea she had enclosed in eye.

135. The Painter Munch

The painter caught the dumb mouth,
Fixed wide, in a man out walking
Down a road. One moment past,
Pleasantly, he was musing,
With the sun shining south
Behind him. Air and hill
Were drawn together
In blue and green paste
When the painted mouth is stilled.
Afflicted by knottier
Pigment, the eye, off-guard,
Suffers and goes mad,
In rigor mortis.

136. Words for Father

Now you are ill,
the body has broken down
after the hot decades of labour.
now is sudden time
to rest with restless muscles,
to close the eyes of responsibility.
fate is not kind,
generosity made you no rich man,
nor too much kindness a healer for heartbreaks.
after the years, the hot sun
over the dry whitening head,
the evenings that drained life out of you,
the debts of duty,
you are home, on a hard bed
out of sleep, when you need sleep most.
the sons and the daughters
are young, you have married late
and we are young to an old father
me, i have pulled out my wet roots
to follow a dry road
the way home is a long lane
lost in the undergrowth.
home was not the kind of love i seek,
not knowing its doors or windows,
being left only with a fragmented past,
which unwise affairs broke
through the brittle centre.
i was too broken to care
though i know that not to care

was the sin of the rootless runner.
your eldest daughter married,
she does not understand the web of male worries.
the other children are too young
to know your circular chase of disappointment
now you are ill,
the good God return you the breath of your youth
for you have been born to be young,
to stand and fight through the days
and the rude elements.
is your traitor in the blood.
but father, it is time to rest now
to close your eyes on the world,
to feel the luxury of the holidays
that you never took
that have collected into one sickness.
now that you are ill,
leave the worries to the young,
the world is too difficult now,
too fast against the slow blood
of an old man
close your red eyes now
and go to sleep.
this illness will go with the heat.
when you wake up
we shall be around
to see the youth in your eyes
and body and voice.

MOHAMMED HAJI SALLEH
(1942-)

He was a Malaysian poet and writer. Born in a village called Temerick, Trong, British Malaya. He soon moved to Sungai Acheh Penang where he had his schooling and graduated from Malaya College. He further studied in Universiti Sains, Malayaisa. He became a professor emeritus in English in the same university. His main collections of poems are- *Pantun: The PoetryofPassion*(2019), *Kamabara MenchariSampadan*(2019), *The GenealogyofKings*and *SeekingHang Tuah* (2019).

137. Blood

The blood in me has travelled so many centuries,
flowed in unknown veins
across swampy rivers and proud straits.
the loins that have borne the beginnings that were me
are so distant and divorced from these wild wild
thoughts.
the great-grandfather who walked in piety
had filtered his purity into his dutch-hating son
who walked with him and with god.
they who have dominated their communities had
traditions;
purified the ancestral mud to clean cultivable earth and
grew in its clutch children of faith and contentment but
the blood has collected corruptions in the new arteries
torn from the river.
much as I owe, I am.
they have slept without knowing me
and I shall sleep in the same ignorance.
how foreign are these stalks that share the same roots.
my sister has diluted my blood in another's,
uncles and aunts have forgotten me before their
children.
I have come to an isolation
where thoughts are not coloured by blood.
the link is loose, worn weak by careless time.
my children live in the grasp of the present
where only the present preoccupies,
like me, they forget the chains that from the past bind
them.

the present is too crowded.

E. E. TIANG HONG (1933-1990)

He was a Malayan poet of Chinese ancestry. Born at Malacca during the British Colonial Period. He is known as one of the outstanding poets of the first generation of Malyan poets in English. His first book of Poetry appeared in 1960. He was extremely disturbed by the political developments in the newly independent Malaysia. He died by cancer in 1990. His main collections are- *Tengaara* Focus, and *If of the My Face.*

138. On Writing a Poem

To be simple is not a simple thing,
Not simply a matter of letting words
Speak for themselves, being grown-up,
Who will not easily take to being
Ordered about, or chaperoned,
Dressed up like dolls
And smart soldier boys
For a debut at a regimental ball.
How to control these diverse selves
Who will not willingly conform
For all the coaxing and the threats
To have nothing more to do with them all,
To gather the sparks of energy,
Marshal them to the heat of a tempo,
How to restrain the Master Self himself
Who will insist on projecting his own Ego
Is more that a trick on a tightrope,
Finding a parallelogram's Resultant,
or setting one faction Against another—a matter of
practice.
To be simple is to be involved
In a whole chaos, the claims and counterclaims
Of mind, heart, word, a universe
On fire-and the final sacrifice.

EDWIN THUMBOO (1933-)

He was a famous Singaporean poet, critic and academic. He was born in
Singapore. His father was Tamil Indian school-teacher and mother,
Teochew Peranakam Chinese Housewife. He graduated from the
University of Malay in 1956. Because he rejected for selection as teacher
in university, he served in Civil Service for nine years, before going to
University. He received a Ph.D. in 1970. His main collections of poems
are- *RibofEarth*(1956), *Gods Can Die*(1977) *Fried: Poems*(2003)
StillTravelling(2008).

139. The Exile

He was not made for politics,
For change of principles
Unhappy days, major sacrifice.
Even a bit part in a tragedy
Seemed most unlikely.
There was in him a cool Confucian smile.
Some suitable history would have been
A place in the Family Bank,
Consolidated by a careful match,
A notable gain in family wealth,
A strengthening of the Clan.
An ordinary life, ordinary longevity.
Of these things his father sadly dreams.
He was not made for politics. But those
days were China-wrought, Uncertain of loyalties,
full of the search For a soul, a pride
Out of ancestral agony, gunboat policy,
The nation's breaking up,
The disaster of the Kuomintang.
So the new people took him in
To cells, discussions, exciting oratory,
Gave him a cause.
Work quietly, multiply the cells
Prepare for the bloom of a hundred flowers.
The flowers came, fast withereth too.
Made conspicuous by principles
And the discipline of the group,
He thought to stand his ground, defy the law.
Re-actionaries he said.

And so he stood in the dock.
Many documents were read. Those who planned
The demonstration, allotted tasks
Had run to fight another day—they had important work,
Could not be spared, were needed to arrange
More demonstrations.
Impersonally, the verdict was
Exile to the motherland,
A new reality.
He stood pale, not brave, not made for politics.

140. Gods Can die

I have seen powerful men
Undo themselves, keep two realities
One for minor friends, one for the powers that be,
The really powerful. Such people take a role
Supporting managers of state,
Accept an essential part in some minor project.
But after a bit of duty,
That makes them fester with intentions,
They play the major figure to old friends.
We understand and try to seek a balance in the dark
To know the private from the public monument,
To find our way between the private and the public
argument
Or what *can* be said or if a thing is meant
Or meant to make amends? is generous or mean?
The casual word, the easiness, the quick straight answer,
The humane delay, the lack of cautiousness
That gave ample laughter to our evenings
Are too simple for these days of power
Whose nature is to hint not state.
So when one has a chance to talk the conversation
Hesitates on the brink of momentous things;
He ponders...
Suggesting by some unremark There was much more to
be said.
It's a pity: good men who seek to serve
Bind themselves unto a cause,
Then use the fate of nations as a rationale
To take their friends aside,

To lead themselves into some history,
We gain uncertain statesmen: many lose a friend.
But I am glad that others are powerful with compassion,
Who see before we do what troubles us
And help in kindness, take ignorance in tow.
If not for such we lose our gods
Who lived but now are dying in our friends.

141. Words

Words are dangerous, especially
The simple kind you leave behind for others,
For undesirable relatives and assorted purposes.
They are understood simply, edited,
Taken with a kind of air, a careful disregard:
Their plainness complicates.
When you say 'Tell him please,
That the anger has come to pass
That friendship is not maimed...or
Please do come but after the
Fever has been put aside...'
When you mean to be polite,
Careful, explicit, considerate, circumspect,
Adopting the proper tone,
You are likely to be quoted as saying
'He won't...'
Words are neither valid, merciful nor bad,
In themselves, nothing unless used, urged,
Imported into dialogue,
Becoming part-anger, part-laughter, bruised,
Adding to the mood and gesture.
Words are words. Except for us
They are not personalities.

142. Ulysses by the Merlin

I have sailed many waters,
Skirted islands of fire,
Contended with Circe
Who loved the squeal of pigs;
Passed Scylla and Charybdis
To seven years with Calypso,
Heaved in battle against the gods.
Beneath it all
I kept faith with Ithaca, travelled,
Travelled and travelled, Suffering much,
enjoying a little;
Met strange people singing
New myths; made myths myself.
But this lion of the sea
Salt-maned, scaly, wondrous of tail,
Touched with power, insistent
On this brief promontory ... Puzzles.
Nothing, nothing in my days
Foreshadowed this
Half-beast, half-fish,
This powerful creature of land and sea.
Peoples settled here, Brought to this island
The bounty of these seas, Built towers topless as Ilium's.
They make, they serve, They buy, they sell.
Despite unequal ways, Together they mutate,
Explore the edges of harmony, Search for a centre;
Have changed their gods,
Kept some memory of their race In prayer, laughter, the way
Their women dress and greet.

They hold the bright, the beautiful,
Good ancestral dreams
Within new visions, So shining,
urgent, Full of what is now.
Perhaps having dealt in things,
Surfeited on them,
Their spirits yearn again for images,
Adding to the dragon, phoenix,
Garuda, naga, those horses of the sun,
This lion of the sea,
This image of themselves.

KIRPAL SINGH (1894-1974)

He was a spiritual master (*satguru*)in the tradition of Radha Soami. Born in Sayyd Kasran, Punjab which is now in Pakistan. He lived in Lahore during the period of his discipleship and attained the position of Deputy Comptroller of Military Accounts. He was awarded with the Padma Visbhushan. His main collections of poems are-*The Man I know Thyself* (1954), *A Crown of Life: A Study in Yoga* (1961)*Naam or Word* (1970) and *Ruhani Satsang* (1973), and *Morning Talks*(1974).

143. To a Visitor to Singapore

You come to my country loaded with your riches
We offer you a convenient stop
allow you to tempt us, lure our pretty girls
corrupt our innocence
because we need your money to survive.
back home you describe our clean and efficient city
but our politics you despise
say our way of life is stifling, oppressive
yet again and again you return
thriving on our survival's need
I often wonder what comfort
you derive from this amazing compromise

144. Change

My world has changed,
keeps changing,
where is that temple
I went to with my granny?
where is the school
where I broke records?
time, you've undone me
you came so fast
I could not believe
my experience was so short-lived.

YASMINE GOONERATNE
(1935-)

She was a Sri Lankan poet, short story writer, critic, university professor and essayist. She did her B.A. from Bishop College, university of Ceylon and later she studied in Cambridge University, Cambridge, England. She is married to Sri Lankan physician Dr.Bredon Gooneratne. She served in Macquerie University, Sydney. He works are- *A Change of Skies* (1991), *SweetandSimpleKind*(2006), *ThePleasuresof Conquest* (1995). For her literary contribution she is awarded with The Order of Australia.

145. On an Asian Poet Fallen Among American Translators

My world has changed,
Two hundred years.
Time enough to build an empire or
build a nation but a span too brief it seems
for the building of craft or courtesy, shaping of skills.
That Puritan grimace to begin with—
death in the heart, and in the loins where poetry
takes birth and breath a gaping emptiness under
layer on layer of tenuous talent, brash gestures,
a spreading taste for the macabre.
There is death in your touch America.
Hold no cigarette to our lips
Do not light up your
maudlin dreams
with cryings out of our names
"Do you hear me? Are you there?"
We are not there, never have been
nor ever shall. Take
your hand off our shoulders
our names from your computerized prize lists
and your leprous fingers off
our poetry.
No wonder Eliot ran away from you and Pound went
crazy
Turning away from your deserts Frost found a small
satisfaction then fell silent.
Here and there

is "one who gathers samphire—dreadful trade'
Lingering on the shores of childhood some wait,
hoping the tide will turn bringing in more than
driftwood and broken stones.
Others try to save something of the past
searching diligently among shards
and rubble for possible images.
America
empty of grace
graveyard of art
monster
living on lazar-house know-how
and hot-house pretensions
America, new found land
long lost, it seems, to poetry

146. There was a Country

There was a country where fine poems lay
close to the surface. Under every hedge
each passing shower would bare a glittering edge.
No stream but, sifted, yielded poetry.
I kicked a stone aside in irritation
and saw its under—surface start to gleam
and there beneath my feet there waited seams
so rich, the merest movement brought creation.
Here it is not the same. Though poetry
occurs, they say, I have not glimpsed it yet,
stumbled upon or caught it in a net of words.
I feel that poems here must lie
Deeper than opals, deeper far than oil
and all the tools I am accustomed to —love,
anger, pity, wit-will hardly do,
blunt as this air has made them, for such toil.
There was a country where, when sorrow grazed
the heart but once the Muse brought forth her
plenty to twos and fours, half-dozens, dozens,
twenties. The mine seemed inexhaustible, a dazed
Discoverer, wondering, merely poured them
down on paper. Grief would need to strike so
deep here, that I'd rather let creation sleep
than mine the diamonds for a poet's crown.

LAKDASA WIKKRAMA SINHA(1941-1978)

He was a famous Sri Lankan poet who wrote both in English and Sinhalese languages. He is widely known for his fusion of Western and South Asian literary traditions in his poetry. He studied at St.Thomas College, Mount Lavinia, Sri Lanka. He published his collections privately. His main collections are -*Lustre:Poems*(1965), *JanakiharanaandOther Poems*(1967), *FifteenPoems*(1970), and *TheGrasshopper Gleaming* (1976).

147. Don't Talk to Me About Matisse

Don't talk to me about Matisse, don't talk to me
about Gauguin, or even
the earless painter Van Gogh,
& the woman reclining on a blood-spread...
the aboriginal shot by the great white hunter Matisse
with a gun with two nostrils, the aboriginal
crucified by Gauguin—the syphilis-spreader, the yellowed.
obesity.
Don't talk to me about Matisse.
the European style of 1900, the tradition of the studio
where the nude woman reclines forever
on a sheet of blood.
Talk to me instead of the culture generally—
how the murderers were sustained
by the beauty robbed of savages: to our remote
villages the painters came, and our white-washed
mud-huts were splattered with gunfire.

PATRICK FERNANDO
(1931-1983)

He was another Sri Lankan poet who served as a tax officer in the Revenue Department (1952-79). He was born in Sri Lanka and raised there. He is known as the most accomplished and polished poets of Sri Lanka. His collection of poems is- *London too* (1955).

148. Elegy for My Son

There must be some terrible power
In the earth and wind and sunshine
How else could the young tree,
A favourite of these three
Sicken in a single day and die?
And I who took some pride over
Planting and tending it
And caught its assent to life
The sun's and wind's keen sponsorship of
This fine young tree, more admiring than proud.
There must be some strange excess of love
In earth and wind and sun that
With notice of just a little day
Took such a fine young tree away.
Whenever I stand in the empty place,
thoughts Brandished wildly sign and sing in memory.
Earth, wind and sun go about their work
As if nothing has occurred,
Calm as conspirators after the deed
Driving me to almost believe nothing
Has happened. I am the tree that's gone,
That tree and I being one.

JEAN ARASANAYAGAM
(1931-2019)

She was a famous Sri Lankan poet and a passionate teacher of English. The youngest of the three children to her parents whose ancestry was Dutch. She was called a Dutch Burgher. She grew up and spent her life in Kandy. Attended Girls' High School, and later education local college and M.A. in Strathclyde University U.K. visiting fellow to Exter University, Scotland. Her works are- *ColonialInheritanceand OtherPoems*(1984), *Kindura* (1973), *Poems of Season Beginning and a Season Over*(1977) and *Water Flows Clear and the Shooting of Floricans*(1993) and *CryoftheKite*(1984).

149. In the Month of July

Childhood is far away
Beneath a tree
playing with pebbles
skillfully tossing them from
back of hand
to palm
requiring a certain skill and
magical ritualistic incantations
As one grows older
the pebbles grow too into great stones and
rocks hurled with violence smashed
skulls spilled brains splattering the pavements
In the month of July
a man fled from his pursuers
he climbed a tree
the mob aimed stones at him
Until they got him down
probably fell off, his grasp loosened
slippery with blood, his body already battered
and then they trampled him to death.

KAMALA WIJERATNE (1939-)

She was a famous Sri Lanka poetess. She was born in Ulapane, a small village near Kandy, Sri Lanka. She was educated in the field of English, a short story writer and poet. She got educated at Teldeniya and graduated from St.Scholastics College, Kandy in 1955 and also in Madya Mahavidyalaya, Gampala, in 1958. She has a P.G.Diploma from the University of Ceylon and later an M.A., from the University of Edinburgh. Her main collections are - *The Smell of Araliya* (1983), *A House Divided*(1985), *TheWhiteSareeandOtherPoems*(1988), *MilleniumPoems* (2002), and *My Green Book* (2015).

150. On Seeing a White Flag Across a By - Road

Only that white flag
bedraggled
rain-sodden,
announces your arrival
The sealed box
has defied
all identity;
has even stopped
speculation
about the way you died.
Your mother,
shocked benumbed,
whimpers in dull agony.
Your sister her years
crippled Stoops by the
dimming candle.
You, who fought for king and country
where are your plaudits?
where are the flowers?
where are the banners?
A bluebottle wails a panegyric.
Your comrades locked in struggle,
have their duty performed;
They brought you home, to lie in a familiar loam.
The nation has saluted you without
haggle, rest you now in heavenly peace.
From your neighbour's house

blares the cricket news,
They drink Coca Cola and sit around:
the screen has gazers mesmerized
and they loll spell-bound;
from your compound's end
popular music expletes.
Crackers explode:
It is the next door neighbour's
betrothal; the reception's at the
Intercontiental.
the bluebottle hovers lovingly.
The candle waves unsure the light
etches silhouettes, people file past
your bier they will bury you at sunset.

151. To A student

I know why your eyes leap away
When they meet mine,
Why they quickly stray
From their quiet contact.
I do know your ears are stopped
Against my voice.
The echoes of gun-shots have blocked
All extraneous sound, Blasts of grenades
have cracked the drums,
(You fear for brother, friend and lover.)
My eyes as they see yours
See torn pieces of human flesh,
Suspended from bushes and trees;
Fragments of splintered bones,
Shreds of olive green;
The roads spewing human blood.
My ears echo burst of landmine.
(I tremble for men of kindred blood.)
But why can't your irises lock with mine?
Our ears stop all unkind sound?
Let us shake off these brand names
And search for a herb that heals,
And make a cooling poultice to cure mass lunacy.
Leave behind those Ilions and Carthages
to antique dealers, Let us plan fresh
methodology to stop other Hiroshimas.

ASHLEY HALPE (1967-)

He was a professor of English and a benefactor of humanity. He was a poet writer, and playwright. He was a quintessential Peradinian. He translated a novel under the title *The Way of Lotus* (1985) He held a chair in the University of Ceylon, Peradiniya, and also a Fellow of the Cambridge University. His main collections are- Waiting for the Bells (2013), Siligiri Poems, and Silent Arbiter.

152. The Boyhood of Chittha

Chittha was born to many benedictions.
His fondest, gay in hope,
set to shape his glory,
foreboding nothing.
They made him two miraculous toys:
one, pliant with story, ready with curious noise
of serpent, parrot, garudha, or bear;
the other warm, circumambient,
pillow in sickness (he was often ill).
They created him gentle, seemly in will,
swayed by a kiss. Nor was denied
the rod,but tenderly, thoughtfully applied.
And—n.b.—there was a servant
vatic with childish fancy. He
wove in the colours of his yokel mind
legends of god and hero, beast and tree:
Gemunu, tearing out brilliant ear-rings
for the starved monk, reeked copious blood
on golden shoulder-blades; his famous elephant
was huge as a double-decker, wise as father;
and Yasodhara blushed in every breeze,
so fine her noble skin. Behind the trees
behind the garden wall toothed demons lurked:
the servant, not surprisingly, was sacked.
And so to Robin Hood, Drake-filled Devon,
Prince Arthur, and Lancelot of the Lake,
(Abridged and Simplified). At seven
he versified—after a fashion—
Horatius, Columbus, the evening star. Ere eleven

he'd laid violent hands on libraries—or digests
would drop tit-bits re Scott or Charlemagne.
At fifteen, late for these climes, the pain
of childhood ended, the sudden ecstasies
of fierce tenderness for some female child.
Stirred by this spirit, appalled
by the loveless, smiting old arch-Hebrew
he felt battered, shattered, a jack-joke,
read much, learnt Young Togetherness,and how to
smoke;
yet, through penumbral nights, his soul
emerged chastened, whole
and Peradeniya claimed him for her own.

153. From the New World for William Hull

Finding, at our furthest point, on our widest arc,
ost in Manhattan, or mired in the of
Midwestern mediocrity,
the still voices speak to the still
remembering blood bearing a hush of
wind upon dusty leaves, a ripple of chattery birds,
or even the shadow of one dead in our absence.
The Winter bites, as slow
November mocked our unseasonable blood,
Spring's parade amuses, for we foreknow
disastrous heavy Summer, thunderstorms,
iced tea, floss, freckles, festivals, Bermuda shorts
we know it's hard days at home; hard hands
heave and in their heaving are
indifferent to our troubled solicitude
fools prosper, rains do not come or
come too soon, anxious eyes watch
clouds low over the sea or some blank bureaucrat
assigning hope or despair; and, to be entirely frank,
as we lay hip to hip and palm to breast we do not think
what constellations gleam above the bed
These provisos all made, farewell America
and all your awesome works. Headed home we catch
scents of New Year cooking across half the world.

CHAND R. SIRIMANNE (1956-)

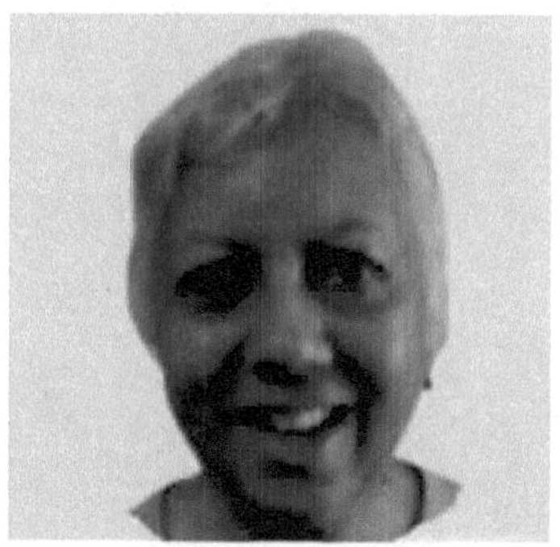

Chand R. Sirimanne was born in Sri Lanka and migrated to Australia in 1990. She has worked as a freelance writer and an ESL instructor for over three decades mainly in Australia but also in Canada and Sri Lanka. Chand currently works as a writer/researcher, and she has written and translated several articles and works on Buddhism. She has an MA in Applied Linguistics from Macquarie University and a PhD from the Department of Studies in Religion, University of Sydney. Chand's doctoral thesis was on The evolving relevance and therapeutic value of the ethico-psychological perspective of the mind-body complex and meditation in Theravâda Buddhism. She has been practicing meditation since 2001.

154. The Uncrossed Bridge

After the morning's hustle and bustle
Chaotic departures of lunch boxes
When our home sighs sadly relieved
Like an empty polished sea shell,
I am drawn unwillingly to your room
Still very much your own
Though you have been gone long
Never to claim ownership again.
Rows and rows of books standing
To attention, even without their commander,
Your finally emptied ash-tray
Still a little ashy to my touch
I try to continue our dialogue
Carried on for thirty years
And to put together the puzzle
That I could not all those years
I ask a thousand questions
Offer ten thousand explanations;
Sorting out happiness and pain, given and received
The untidy jumble of angry love, accusing regrets
Trying in vain to cross that final bridge
Which you still keep drawn up.

NEW ZEALAND

EDWARD TREGEAR (1846-1931)

He was the son of Adolphus Tregear and Caroline Tregear of Rose mount, Province of Quebec, Canada. He wrote and published several collections of poems.

155. The Whetu Plains

A lonely rock above a midnight plain,
A sky whose moonlit darkness flies
No shadow from the 'Children of the Rain',
A stream whose double crescent far-off lies,
And seems to glitter back the silver of skies.
The table-lands stretch step by step below
In giant terraces, their deeper ledges
Banded by blackened swamps (that, near, I know
Convolvulus-entwined) whose whitened edges
Are ghostly silken flags of seeding water-sedges.
All still, all silent, 'tis a songless land,
That hears no music of the nightingale,
No sound of waters falling lone and grand
Through sighing forests to the lower vale,
No whisper in the grass, so wan, and grey, and pale.
When Earth was tottering in its infancy,
This rock, a drop of molten stone, was hurled
And tost on waves of flames like those we see
(Distinctly, though afar) evolved and whirled
A photosphere of fire around the Solar World.
Swift from the central deeps the lightning flare
Piercing the heart of Darkness like a spear,
Hot blasts of steam and vapour thunder'd through
The lurid blackness of the atmosphere.
A million years have passed, and left strange quiet her
Peace, the deep peace of universal death
Enshrouds the kindly mother-earth of old,
The air is dead, and stirs no living breath
To break these awful Silences that hold

The heart within their clutch, and numb the veins with cold.
My soul hath wept for Rest with longing tears,
Called it 'the perfect crown of human life'-
But now I shudder lest the coming years
Should be with these most gloomy terrors rife;
When palsied arms drop down outwearied with the strife.
May Age conduct me by a gentle hand
Beneath the shadows ever brooding o'er
The solemn twilight of the Evening Land,
Where man's discordant voices pierce no more,
But sleeping waters dream along a sleeping shore.
When I, when Youth has spent its fiery strength
And flickers low, may rest in quietness
Till on my waiting brow there falls at length
The deeper calm of the Death-Angel's kiss -
But not, oh God, such peace, such ghastly peace as this.

KATHERINE MANSFIELD (1888-1923)

Katherine Mansfield was a famous poet and short story writer from New Zealand. She was a writer and essayist and the most influential writer of the modernist movement in New Zealand literature. She was born and raised in a house on Tinakori Road in the Wellington suburbia of Thorndon. She was the third child in the Beauchamp family. She attended Wellington Girls's College and has been called Maata Mahapuku. She published several collections of stories and poems. *Poems*(1923) is the best known of her works. She died in France at the age of 34.

156. The Man with the Wooden Leg

There was a man lived quite near us;
He had a wooden leg and a goldfinch in a green cage.
His name was Farkey Anderson,
And he'd been in a war to get his leg.
We were very sad about him,
Because he had such a beautiful smile
And was such a big man to live in a very small house.
When he walked on the road his leg did not matter
so much;
But when he walked in his little house
It made an ugly noise.
Little Brother said his goldfinch sang the loudest of
all birds,
So that he should not hear his poor leg
And feel too sorry about it.

A. R. D. FAIRBURN (1904-57)

He was a famous writer, artist and poet. He was born and died in Auckland. He was also known as Rex. His grandfather William Thomas Fairburn was a surveyor who came as a missionary to New Zealand. He attended Auckland Grammar School and later Elam School of Art and University of Auckland. He was initially influenced by the Georgian poets of England. His main works are- *Poems1929-41*, *Walking on My Feet* (1945), *PoetryHarbinger*and *StrangeRendezview*.

157. Full Fathom Five

He was such a curious lover of shells
and the hallucinations of water
that he could never return out of the sea
without first having to settle a mermaid's bill.
Groping along the sea-bottom of the age
he discovered many particulars he did not care to speak about
even in the company of water-diviners
things sad and unspeakable
moss-covered skulls with bodies fluttering inside
with the unreality of specks moving before the eyes of a
photograph
trumpets tossed from the decks of ocean-going liners
eccentric starfish fallen from impossible heavens
fretting on uncharted rocks
still continents with trees and houses like a child's drawing
and in every cupboard of the ocean
weary dolphins trapped in honey-coloured cobwebs
murmuring to the revolution Will you be long.
He was happy down there under the frothing ship-lanes
because nobody ever bothered him with statistics
or talk of yet another dimension of the mind.
And eventually and tragically finding he could not drown
he submitted himself to the judgment of the desert
and was devoured by man-eating ants
with a rainbow of silence branching from his lips.

158. Epithalamium

He was such a curious lover of shells
We have found our peace, and move with a turning globe;
the night is all about us, the lovers' robe.
Mortal my love, my strength: your beauty their wound.
Strip quickly darling, your fingers be the wind
undressing a snowy peak to the sun's love,
scatter your clouds, be Everest, O my Eve.
Leap on the bed, lie still, your body truth become dream
torturing my arms before their kingdom come.
Give the wise their negations, the moralists their maps;
our empire the moment, the geometer's point where all shapes
of delight are hidden as joy sleeps in the vine.
I tell you again, what the poor have always known,
that this is all the heaven we shall ever find
in all our footsore and fatal journey and beyond,
and we shall never have enough to keep out foul weather,
or to eke out age, will perish forgetful of each other,
yet breeding saints or subduing Asia set against this
were violating our lives with littleness.
Now at the brink of being, in our pride of blood
let us remember lost lovers, think of the dead
who have no power, who aching in earth lie,
the million bones, white longings in the night of eternity.
O love, how many of our faith have fallen!
Endless the torrent of time, endless and swollen
with tributaries from the broken veins of lovers.
I kiss you in remembrance of all true believers.
Midnight thoughts. Dark garlands to adorn your flesh
so it shine like snow, like fire. Flakes of ash

blowing from doom's far hill. Such wisps of terror
gazed at too long even in your body's mirror
would disrupt our continent, drain our seas,
bring all to nothing. Love, let us laugh and kiss,
only your lips but not with speech can tell
moving in the darkness what is unspeakable,
and though your eyes reflect spring's green and yellow
like a pool
I cannot see them, can only guess at what is more
beautiful
than home at last, than a child's sleep, more full of pity
and gentleness than snow falling on a burning city.

159. I'm Older than you, Please Listen

To the young man I would say:
Get out! Look sharp, my boy,
before the roots are down,
before the equations are struck,
before a face or a landscape
has power to shape or destroy.
This land is a lump without leaven,
a body that has no nerves.
Don't be content to live in
a sort of second-grade heaven
with first-grade butter, fresh air,
and paper in every toilet;
becoming a butt for the malice
of those who have stayed and soured,
staying in turn to sour,
to smile, and savage the young.
If you're enterprising and able,
smuggle your talents away,
hawk them in livelier markets
where people are willing to pay.
If you have no stomach for roughage,
if patience isn't your religion,
if you must have sherry with your bitters,
if money and fame are your pigeon,
if you feel that you need success
and long for a good address,
don't anchor here in the desert—

the fishing isn't so good:
take a ticket for Megalopolis,
don't stay in this neighbourhood!

ALLEN CURNOW (1911-2001)

He was a poet and journalist. He studied in the University of Canterbury, and University of Auckland. He was born in Timaru in 1911, New Zealand and the son of the fourth generation of New Zealand, an Anglican clergyman. He worked with *New Zealand Herald*, the newspaper.He grew up in the religious family. He published nearly thirty collections of poems of which *Collected Poems* (1974) *Continuum: New and LaterPoems* (1972-1988), *RecentPoems*(1941), *Poems-1949-57* (1957), *SelectedPoems* (1990).

160. Time

I am the nor'west air nosing among the pines
I am the water-race and the rust on railway lines
I am the mileage recorded on the yellow signs.
I am dust, I am distance, I am lupins back of the beach
I am the sums the sole-charge teachers teach
I am cows called to milking and the magpie's screech
I am nine o'clock in the morning when the office is clean
I am the slap of the belting and the smell of the machine
I am the place in the park where the lovers where seen.
I am the recurrent music the children hear
I am the level noises in the remembering ear
I am the sawmill and the passionate second gear.
I, Time, am all these, yet exist Among my mountainous
fabrics like a mist, So do they measurable world resist.
I, Time, call down, condense, confer
On the willing memory the shapes these were:
I, more than your conscious carrier, Am island,
am sea, am father, farm, and friend Though
I am here all things my coming attend;
I am, you have heard it, the Beginning and the End.

161. House and Land

Wasn't this the site, asked the historian,
Of the original homestead?
Couldn't tell you, said the cowman;
I just live here, he said, Working for old
Miss Wilson Since the old man's been dead.
Moping under the bluegums
The dog trailed his chain
From the privy as far as the fowl house
And back to the privy again,
Feeling the stagnant afternoon
Quicken with the smell of rain.
There sat old Miss Wilson, With her pictures on the wall,
The baronet uncle, mother's side,
And one she called The Hall; Taking tea from a silver pot
For fear the house might fall.
People in the *colonies,* she said,
Can't quite understand... Why,
from Waiau to the mountains
It was all father's land.
She's all of eighty said the cowman,
Down at the milking-shed.
I'm leaving here next winter.
Too bloody quiet, he said.
The spirit of exile, wrote the historian,
Is strong in the people still.
He reminds me rather, said Miss Wilson,
Of Harriet's youngest, Will.
The cowman, home from the shed, went drinking
With the rabbiter home from the hill.

The sensitive nor'west afternoon
Collapsed, and the rain came;
The dog crept into his barrel
Looking lost and lame.
But you can't attribute to either
Awareness of what great gloom
Stands in a land of settlers
With never a soul at home.

JAMES BAXTER (1926-1972)

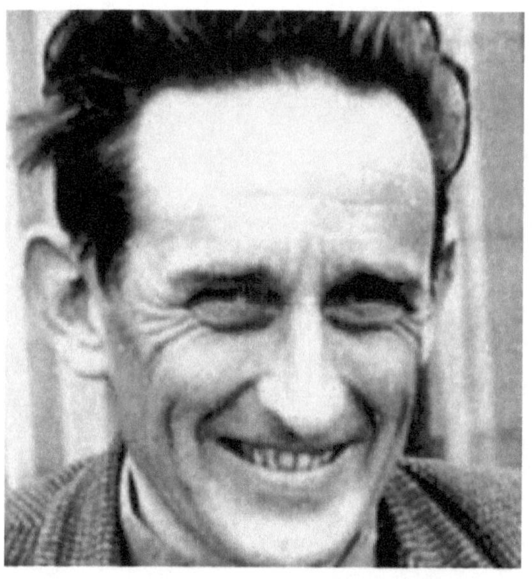

He was a famous New Zealand poet and playwright. Hew as born in Dunedin, as the second child to Archibald Baxter and Millicent Brown.He studied mainly in the University of Sydney and University of Cambridge. He was also known as activist for the preservation of Maori culture. He was one of the New Zealand's most well-known and controversial literary figures. His works are- *ChosenPoems* (1958), *A Selection of Poetry* (1964), *PoemsUnpleasant*(1952), *Jerusalem Sonnets*(1970), *Autumn Testament* (1972) and *Selected Poems*(2009),*Collected Poems*.

162. Pig Island Letters

Stat crux dum volvitur orbis: *
I will sing
can I let you in? The time for talk has gone;
A mountain is the threshold stone
'Mother, I come alone. No books, no bread
Are left in my swag.'
'Why are your hands not clean?'
'There was no soap in the whole damned town.' '
God's grace has need of man's apology.'
"Your face is my theology.'
'Yes; but I gave you a jewel to bring.'
'In the thick gorse of the gully I lost your signet ring.'
'Why should I listen then?'
'On Skull Hill there was none,
No scapular, no sign,
Only the words, / *thirst,*
When the blood of a convict burst
From the body of your son.'
'You may come in.'
Is it like that? At least I know no better;
After a night of argument Mythical, theological,
political, Somebody has the sense to get a boat
And row out towards the crayfish rocks Where,
diving deep, the downward swimmer
Finds fresh water rising up,
A mounded water breast, a fountain,
An invisible tree whose roots cannot be found;
As that wild nymph of water rises
So does the God in man.

Brother Ass, Brother Ass, you are full of fancies,
You want this and that—a woman, a thistle,
A poem, a coffeebreak, a white bed, no crabs;
And now you complain of the weight of the Rider
Who will set you free to gallop in the light of the sun!
Ah well,, kick Him off then, and see how you go
Lame-footed in the brambles; your disconsolate bray
Is ugly in my ears—long ago, long ago,
The battle was fougnt and the issue decided
As to who would be King—go on, little donkey
Saddled and bridled by the Master of the world,
Be glad you can distinguish not an inch of the track.
That the stones are sharp, that your hide can itch,
That His true weight is heavy on your back.

GORDON CHALLIS (1932-2018)

Born in Birmingham, England and raised there. He was a New Zealand poet. He studied in Victoria University college in Wellington in 1950se.It is there where he began to write poetry. He worked as a psychiatrist social worker in Porirua Hospital and emigrated in to New Zealand in 1953. His lived his last days in the Golden Bay. *The Postman*, *The Other Side of theBrain*(2003), *Luck of the Bounce* (2009) and *Building*(1963) are his widely known works.

163. The Postman

This cargo of confessions, messages,
demands to pay, seems none of my concern;
you could say I'm sort of go-between
for abstract agents trusting wheels will turn,
for censored voices stilled in space
Some people stop me for a special letter;
one or two will tell me, if if s fine, that
I have picked the right job for this kind of weather.
A boy who understands life somewhat better asks
where postmen live—if not our office, why?
The work is quite routine but kindnesses
and awkward problems crop up now and then:
one old lady sometimes startles passers-by
claiming she is blameless as she hisses at
people present in her reminiscent ken;
she startled me as well the other day,
gave me a glass of lemonade and slipped
me a letter to deliver—'Don't you say
a word to anyone, if s no concern
of theirs, or yours.' Nor no more it was, except
here was this letter plainly marked 'To God'
and therefore insufficiently addressed.
I cannot stamp it now 'Return to sender'
for addressee and sender may be One. The best
thing is burn it, to a black rose He'll remember.

164. The Thermostatic Man

The world could fall to pieces any moment now;
with luck it won't,
mainly because it hasn't yet. Though cracks appear,
I'll merely count
them leeway spaces left so masses may expand
to meet and don't.
But I, who used to walk bold upright, this day bow
as meek as wheat:
how can I be sure I shall not always fear
to face fierce heat,
to face the sun, not watch my shadow lagging back behind,
and feel complete?
From strips of many metals am I made.
I grow beneath the sun
unevenly. I cannot cry lest the least
tear should cool down one
soft element and strain the others.
I am bland, bend to become
the thermostat which keeps my spirit burning low.
One day I shall
perhaps be tried by a more humble,
human fire which, blending all
my elements in one alloy,
will let me stand upright, ready to fall.

PAKISTAN AND BANGLADESH

KISHWAR NAHEED (1940-)

She was a famous feminist Urdu poetess and a writer from Pakistan. She was born in 1940 in Bulandshehr and was a witness to the Patition violence. She studied in Aligarh Muslim Unviersity. She had a degree in Urdu and learned Persian Language also. She has published several poetry books. Also she has received awards including Sitara-e-Imitiaz for her literary contribution towards Urdu literature. *Lab-I- goya* (1968) *Warq,warqAina*(2006) and *Chand-ki- Bet*i (2012). Her collections are main poetical works.

165. Talking to Myself

Punish me for I've written the significance of the dream
in my own blood written a book ridden with an obsession
Punish me for I have spent my life sanctifying the dream of the future
spent it enduring the tribulations of the night
Punish me for I have imparted knowledge and the skills of the sword
to the murderer and demonstrated the power of the pen to the mind
Punish me for I have been the challenger of the crucifix of hatred
I'm the glow of torches which burn against the wind
Punish me for I have freed womanhood from the insanity of the deluded night
Punish me for if I live you might lose face
Punish for if my sons raise their hands you will meet your end
If only one sword unsheaths itself to speak you will meet your end
Punish me for I love the new life with every breath
I shall live my life and shall doubly live beyond my life
Punish me for then the sentence of your punishment will end.

166. Censorship

In those times when the camera could not freeze
tyranny forever
only until those times
should you have written
that history
which describes tyranny as valour.
Today, gazing at scenes
transferred on celluloid
one can gauge
what the scene is like
and the sound
when trees are uprooted from the hillsides.
whether you are happy or sad
you must breathe
whether your eyes are open or closed
the scene, its imprint on the mind
does not change.
The trees that stand in the river
always remain wooden
cannot become a crocodile.
For a long time now;
we have stood
on the rooftops of stories
believing this city is ours
The earth beneath the foundations has sunk
but even now we stand
on the rooftops of stories
assuming life to be
the insipid afternoon's wasted alleyways

with their shattered bricks
and gapping fissures.

FAIZ AHMED FAIZ (1911-1984)

He was a Pakistani poet and author of several books in Urdu and Punjabi. He was born in Sialkot, Punjab. He had his B.A. and Urdu inArabic Literature. He was also a leading member of the Communist Party of Pakistan. He served as an aide to Zulfikar Ali, Bhutto, the Prime Minister of Pakistan. Faiz was one of the most celebrated popular writer and influential Urdu writes of the times. His works and ideas remain influential today in Pakistan and beyond. *Subh-e-Azad*i, *Naqsh-eFaryad*i, *Dast-e-Sabah*and *Zindannama.*He was the first Asian to get the Lenin Peace Prize.

167. Nowhere, no Trace Can I Discover

Nowhere, No trace can I discover
Of spilt blood,
not on the murderer's hand nor on his sleeve;
no daggers with red lips nor scarlet-pointed swords.
I see not blots on the dust,
no stains on the walls.
Nowhere, nowhere
does the blood reveal its darkness
Not spilt in grandeur
nor as ritual sacrifice,
it was not shed on the field of battle,
it did not raise a martyr's banner.
Screaming loudly the orphan blood flowed on.
No-one had the time or sense,
none bothered to listen.
No witness, no defence;
the case is closed.
The blood of the downtrodden
seeped mutely into the dust.

168. My Guests

The door opens
on my sadness;
there they come, my guests.
There she is, the evening
to lay a carpet of despair.
There goes the night
to speak of pain to the stars.
Here comes the morning
with its shining scalpel
to open the wound of memory.
Then there is afternoon
hiding whips of flame in its sleeve.
All these are my guests
who come to see me day and night.
But when they come
and when they go,
I do not know.
My thoughts are always
drifting homeward,
holding doubts and suspicions
asking many questions.

169. Loneliness

Has anyone come again, sad heart?
No, there is no-one there.
A wayfarer perhaps?
He'll go elsewhere.
The night has melted into
nothingness, the dim twinkling of
stars has disappeared.
The sleepy lamp falters in the hallway;
the street has fallen asleep, giving up
on travellers. Alien dust
has wiped out all the footprints.
Blow out the lamps,
take away the wine, the glass and bottle.
Lock your dreamless doors! No-one
will come here now no-one no more.

FAHMIDA RIAZ (1945-2018)

She was a famous Urdu writer, translator, poet, and social activist of Pakistan. She was born to a literary family in Meerut, British India. Her father Riaz-ud-Din Ahmed was an educationist who involved in establishing modern education system in Sindh province. She was raised by her mother after her father's death and the family shifted to Hyderabad, India. She knew Sindhi, Urdu, and English. Having informal education, she authored many books in English as well as in Urdu of which some are *Godaavari*, *Khatt-e-Marmuz* and *Kahna e Aab O Gill*, the first translation in rhyme of the Masnavi of Jalaluddin Rumi from Persian into Urdu.Her poetic collections are - *Pathar Ki Jaban*(1967) and *Badan Darida*(1973).

170. Voice of Stone

You met me on this lonely hill;
this is the peak of our meeting, this
the stone of my loyalty, naked, wild, sad and desolate.
For centuries
I have stood, embracing it,
collecting your breath in a torn shawl,
my dress billowing in the wind's cruel current.
Still I cling to the sharp dagger-points of stone
which have pierced so deep into my heart
that my blood has stained everything
but for centuries
I have stood embracing it, embracing it
And I send a message to you
with a soaring bird:
If you could see me,
would you not be happy?
Stones turn to glittering diamonds,
roses grow from stone.

AHMED ALI (1910-1994)

He was a famous Pakistani novelist, short story writer, poet, critic translator, diplomat, and scholar. He was born in Delhi and got his education at the Aligarh Muslim University and later, at Lucknow University. He was a visiting professor at Nanjing University and was sent by the British government. He also served on BBC during World War II. He wrote both in Urdu and English. He was a pioneer of the modern Urdu short story, his works included the short story collection *Angarey*(1932), *HamariGali*(1940), *QuidKahana* (1942), and *Maut se Pehle* (1941). His collections of poems are- *PurpleGoldMountain*(1961), *FirstVoices* (1965), and *Selected Poems*(1988).

171. On the Tenth Night of the Tenth Moon I Walk by the West Lake and Meet Another Me

On the tenth night of tenth moon
I walked by the West Lake contemplating
The wind and clouds. My shadow
Walked ahead of me, another me
Facing my greying head shaking,
Not with palsy, but to attract my gaze.
"Who are you that walk in pursuit of me?"
Said the shadow. "Wherever I go you follow me."
I thought," said I, "that it were you
"Who always walked ahead of me
Or dogged my steps wherever I went.
It's time this pretence came to end."
And I pulled my sword and raised
It in the air to settle for ever this duality.
Empty laughter filled my ears as I cut
The frosty air, my enemy performing The same gesture.
"You are not you, Nor I am I," said he, and opened his arms
Which I put around my neck, and met
Li Po embracing the moon in the Nether
World Across the Yellow Springs.

172. Dialogue with Lee San

When young the thought of death
Had never crossed our minds, Lee San.
We had no time for it; and even when
We sought it in the bitter frustrations of youth,
It was fullness of experience and old-age maturity
We desired and falsely assumed, never thinking
That when we are old and weary and full
Of the sadness of life, no friend
Shall visit us from the past
To keep us company in the loneliness of age.
Perhaps, having passed beyond the circle of death,
You have found the secret of peace in the Nether World.
"Deep under the frozen earth," said Lee San,
"The moss dreams of Summer the Winter long,
And, thrusting the cold crust of snow,
Raises its face towards the light
With patient persistence braving the wind
To make for itself a place in the sun.
Green grow the weeds, the flowers fade away.
Nothing lives, nothing dies: only these
Alternations of night and day
Bring news of the seasons eternally."
But the shame of one's own actions, said I,
And the feeling of regret in the bones at the failure to meet
Life's obligations with life's failing strengths,
And the sense of the guilt of many wrongs,
Of meeting favours with pride, love with arrogance,
Multiplies and remains.
"A man's life," said Lee San, "is like

A frog's in a well that looks at the patch
Of the sky that alone is visible, which he takes
For the universe. We think, so we are.
Cease to think, you will pass beyond being:
To be uncreated, identify."
Alas, said I, the cares of the moment
Fill the vision like the peaks of Tien Shan.
And alas for man's ingratitude!
Bent under the load of years no choice has he
But to bear the burden of insults and the ironies of life.
Can you ask for atonement of wrongs
Done to yourself by your own hand?
"Not so," he replied as he sat on his jade throne,
Pointing to the earth in a gesture of peace.
"The source of right and wrong is the same.
You seek and do not find. So turn from desire
If you wish for poise and tranquillity.
Look at the bamboo and the pine, for ever green,
Filled with the calm of awareness and oneness of being.
You surround yourself with vanities that lead
In the end to a gossamer of cares the spider weaves
Into a web of the dream of passing things,
Prayer without faith, song devoid of song: A lonely line of geese
Flapping its wings across the emptiness of space.
Detract and gather and narrow the circle to the point,
Disperse the caravans bearing
The merchandise of nothing to nothing.
And be ready to embrace
The beginning in the end."

173. The Year of the Rat: 1984

In this Year of the Rat the gopher's granary is full;
Only men die of hunger, greed and hate.
Like the leaves of Autumn falling one by one
The tree of life is being denuded of its dress.
The Year of the Rat revives the call of dead desire
Across the gulf of sun-drained shores, the silent seas,
The fresh foot-prints of love
Seeking the lost imprints of lovers' feet.
In this Year of the Rat one should not die
Celebrating with youthful revellers the
promise of Spring Waving the branches of
weeping-willow, dancing
The tiger dance to the din of loud drums.
When the year comes to an end
Hope will have shed its flowers at the altar of age-god,
And only a shell would remain
Clutching the carious bones of faith.
In the Year of the Rat the last refuge of man
Is life in death.

MAKI KHURESHI (1927-1995)

Maki Khureshi was born in Kolkatta in 1927 in a Parsee family. Her father Lt.Col. Jal Dhunjibhoy was a psychiatrist, who served the elite and the corps. She spent her early life in Ranchi, Bihar She taught at the University of Karachi for thirty years. She wrote in English. Hanif Khureshi, the famous writer, was her nephew. *The Far Thing* is the only best known collection of poems.

174. The Kittens

In this Year of the Rat the
gopher's granary is full;
There are too many kittens.
Even the cat is dismayed
at this overestimation
of her stock and slinks away.
Kind friends cannot adopt them all.
My relatives say: take them
to a bazaar and let them go
each to his destiny. They'll live
off pickings. But they are so small
somebody may step on one
like a tomato.
Or too fastidious to soil a polished
shoe will kick it out of his path.
If they survive the gaunt dogs and
battering heels, they will starve gently,
squealing a little less each day.
The European thing to do is drown them.
Warm water is advised to lessen the shock.
They are so small it takes only a minute.
You hold them down and turn your head away.
Then the water shatters. Your hands
are frantic eels. Oddly
like landed fish, their blunt pink mouths
open and shut. Legs strike out.
Each claw, a delicate nail
paring, is bared.
They are blind and will never

know you did this to them.
The water recomposes itself.
Snagged by two cultures,
which shall I choose?

ALAMGHIR HASHMI (1951-)

He was also known as Aurangazeb Alamghir Hashmi, is an 'English' poet of Pakistan origin. Considered as *avant- garde*, his early and alter works published to considerable critical acclaim and popularity. Being an educator, he was a practicing transnational Humanism and taught in European and Asian Universities. His main collections of poems are - *The OathandAmen*(1976), *Americaisa Punjabi Word* (1979), *An OldChair*(1979), *My Second in Kentucky* (1981), and *Inland and OtherPoems* (1984).

175. Tankas out of time

I

The top black b//
button your supple fingers
play with on your own shirt,
is a compliment, yes, yes,
to the art of necking.

II

The top black b//
button on your blouse so
punctuates the neck—
line, a cat's eye glinting
there on the road between
the hills.

III

I was merely ex-
plaining a sentence, examples
remaining to the
senses: a starlit night
over the shores of Serendip?

IV

The pink butterfly

settles on my sleeve, and
I try not to move.
The sun too is about to set.
All colours will soon be one.

V

You violate the lo-gic of
day and night, infil-trating
my dreams round the clock.
Do come in,
but first take off all that.

VI

Understanding is
so rare, as of the man
who said to his wife
in his Babu Latin: "Please
come quick, I'm getting late."

VII

I don't believe it,
only translate. For belief
will get me into
bed with trouble. I'd rather
be spent without the desire.

VIII

You serve an apple-wine.
Your eyes are a sunrise

over the ocean.
We discuss grammar;
what keeps 'cra-ving' from 'asking for'.

IX

The late wild flowers
are still lovely in the woods.
I must keep looking
at them to know the meaning
of desire and that it isn't.

RAZIA KHAN (1936-2011)

She was a Bangladeshi writer, poet, and educationist. She was also a journalist, theatre actor, and columnist for news papers. She was daughter of Maulvi Tamizuddin Khan, a politician and social activist. She did M.A. in the Univ of Dakha and went ot University of Birmingham, on BCL scholarship for higher studies. Her collections are- *Anukalpa*(1959), *He Mohajibo*n(1983), *Draupadi* (1992 and *Bandi Bihongo.*She was awarded Ekushey Padak in 1997 for her contribution to education by her government.

176. My Daughter's Boy-friend

Importunate knocks on the door
Sending tremors of foreboding
Through the frame; that eyeless
Face, unaware of me, excludes
Me from every consideration
The flesh of my flesh is now to be
Nothing to me any longer;
All those sleepless nights over
The sick infant's cradle;
All the agony of birth and rearing
Are to be nothing; only this
Total omission is palpable.
To have woven such silvery dreams
Around a fragile flower
To be snatched off my branches
By a thoughtless hand
Is a thought I never entertained
When I first swelled with pride
With her in my insides.

177. The Monstrous Biped

The low whimper
Of a street-dog
Hit by an unmindful wagon
Stabs like a knife
Stays with me like a scar
Left by bullets.
The more defenceless
The creature the more
The cruelty; indifference.
If the dog could show his teeth,
Dig them into the eyes of the killer,
He might learn to be human.
The monstrous biped Rides your chest
As soon as you stop to rest;
This constant watch tires me;
I would rather breathe a little
Love, laugh, bask in the sun
And in goodness guaranteed;
Instead I have to point my gun
At men who would have me kneel
At their dirty feet Or
women who would steal
My peace if I stopped to blink.

DAUD KAMAL (1935-1987)

He was a Pakistani poet who wrote most of his work in the English language. He was born in Abbottabad in 1935. His father Chaudhury Mohammed Ali, the Vice chancellor of the University of Peshawar. He got his education in Islamia College, Peshawar, and did his Tripos in the University of Cambridge. He was professor of English in University of Peshawar. His poetry was influenced by modernist English-Managua poets like Ezra Pound, W.B. Yeats and T.S. Eliot. His main collections of poems are- *RemoteBeginning, Compass of Love and Other Poems, Recognitions, Before the Carnations Wither.*

178. Hurricane Lamp

'The Fatality of seeing things too well'.

—Wallace Stevens

Sooner or later
cracks appear on the surface
of things :
clay pitchers, glaciers, human faces.
Water is exempt
and the stone's interior sky.
Jagged edge
of the precipice.
Fire without ashes.
Dreams accumulate and harden into reality.
Carrion crows drink from a rain-puddle.
A few steps away women labourers
carry bricks on their heads. Each star
drowns in its own light.

179. Resilience

'The Unendurable is the Beginning of the Curve of Joy.'
-Djuna Barnes

Sparks
from an old anvil—
desiccated petals of fire—
and the rafters
blackened by generations of smoke.
Don't give up : nothing lasts
longer than what can be
endured Boats on the river
and the flowering almond trees. Love—
cloudless wine— but something is always
lacking. Does man learn by suffering? The night
neither denies nor affirms.
Glimpses (or memories) of perfection—
cusp of the moon.
Fortuitous conjunctions.
The leaf turns with the wind.

ZULFIKAR GHOSE (1935-2022)

He was a a Pakistani American poet, novelist, and essayist, living U.S.A. Born in Sialkot, Punjab and in 1942 the family moved to Mumbai, a Muslim. His father Khwaja Mohammed Ghose was a businessman. Being a Muslim, he graduated from the Keele University, England. He taught Ealing Mead, in London. His works are primarily magical realism blending fantasy and hash realism. His main collections of poems are - *The Loss of India* (1964), *Jets from Orange* (1967), *The Violent West* (1972) and *SelectedPoems*(1991).

180. The Monument to Sibelius in Rio de Janeiro

Driving back from the Botanical Gardens or the Jockey
Club or heading for the tunnel to the city's new
southern zone, you come to a busy intersection
where on a small concrete island there is
a conventional bust of Sibelius reminiscent
of many a supposedly visionary figure—
a renowned scientist, say, or perhaps some shrewd
lean-faced politician, one of those men whose
fixed stare in bronze or marble proclaims
social conscience, altruism, or plain genius,
and whom you pass by without any thought because
Your immediate concern is with making it to
the corner before the lights change. Only the sun
falling on the sunken cheek or on the stony eyes
in a second's perception as determinedly you race
to the corner prompts in your mind the idea of
a statue to a hero and in a fraction of that
second—already gone now with its evocation of
memories and past convictions, a knowledge
of certainty that you've begun to see as a heretical
version of your own former sense of things—
images flash through your mind of monuments
Scattered about the world to men and women
who committed acts of bravery or who represent
a nation's intellectual genius. .In each country
the natives have their own style
of driving competitively past the fixed landmarks.

We need monuments then only in the way
we need a large tree or a bend in the river or
a mountain peak just off the centre of a canvas
in a charming old painting of a lovely or a haunting
landscape, which is to say, in order to perpetuate
an aesthetic preconception. The river and the mountain
remain nameless in such pictures, only their *form*
is to be admired, and similarly the statues of great
heroes become an anonymous blur in our motoring
progression, though their presence at certain corners
reminds us which way we must turn to reach
where we're going. With the monument to Sibelius
I was on foot with cars coming from six directions.
I ran across a gap and stood by the statue
on its island. I was surprised to read the name
Sibelius. Seeing the statue many times before,
always while driving past, I'd thought
the monument must be to some Brazilian hero,
some intrepid explorer of a wild interior.
The lights turned red, the cars stopped, and there
by the curb, a foot away from where I stood
beside Sibelius was a car with its radio playing
popular music and its driver staring grimly
at the lights. I liked Sibelius thirty years ago when
I too might have agreed to commission his bust.
There must be a great redundancy of statues
in the world of people made into monuments
whom a revisionist history casts as villains
or merely as mediocrities and yet whom the traffic
of the living does not distinguish from
the enduring heroes—Simon Bolivar for one,
in the traditional form of the hero, high upon horseback,
solitary commander now of a concrete island:

the cars speed by one of the creators of
South America upon the highway curving round
a famous picture-postcard view of Rio, vaster
numbers charge blindly past in an hour's traffic
than all the armies Bolivar conquered.

Bibliography

Press, John(ed.) *CommonwealthLiterature,*London: Heinemann,1965.

Walsh, William. *Commonwealth Literature*. Oxford Paperbacks, University Series, London: Oxford University Press, 1973.

Walsh, William. (ed.) *ReadingsinCommonwealthLiterature,* Oxford: Clarendon Press, 1973.

Narasimaiah C.D. (ed.) *The Awakened Conscience.* New Delhi: Sterling Publishers, 1978.

*TheJournalofCommonwealthLiterature.*London, Oxford University Press.

Nazareth Peter, *LiteratureandSocietyinModernAfrica*, Nairobi: East African Literature Bureau,1971.

Cape Jack and Kringe, Uys, *The Penguin Book of African Verse*, Harmondsworth: Penguin Books, 1968.

Moore Gerald and Beier Ulli (ed). *Modern Poetry from Africa*, Rev. ed Harmondsworth: Penguin Books, 1970.

Judith Wright, (ed.)*A Book of Australian Verse*, 2$_{nd}$edition, Melbourne: OUP, 1968.

Elliot Brian, *TheLandscapeofAustralianPoetry.*Melbourne: Cheshire, 1967.

AustralianLiteraryStudies, Hobart: University of Tasmania, Biannual.

Atwood, Margaret. (ed.) *An Oxford Book of Canadian Verse*, Toronto: OUP, 1982.

Atwood, Margaret, *Survival:ThematicGuidetoCanadian Literature.* Toronto: OUP,1972.

CanadianLiterature: AQuarterlyofCriticismad Review., Vancouver: Univ.Of British Columbia.

Parthasarathy R..(ed.)*Ten Twentieth Century Indian Poets.* New Delhi: OUP, 1976.

Badiger, V.R. *AnAnthologyofModernIndianEnglishPoetry*. Agra: Current Publications, 2015.

O'Sullivan Vincent,(ed.) *An Anthology of Twentieth Century New ZealandPoetry*. 2nd Edition, Wellington: OUP,1875.

James Lous(ed.). *The Islands in Between: Essays on West Indian Literature*. London: OUP,1968.